THE DESTRUCTION OF LOGIC FROM WITHIN

Matthew M. Kryzanowski

IDEA FACTORY PRESS

Scarborough Canada

Experiments in Christian Thought Volume 1

The Destruction of Logic from Within

Christian Spiritual Fulfillment as a Function of Conscious Awareness & Free Will

Matthew M Kryzanowski

Idea Factory Press
Scarborough Canada
https://www.ideafactorypress.com

The Destruction of Logic from Within
Christian Spiritual Fulfillment as a Function of Conscious Awareness and Free Will
Experiments in Christian Thought, Volume 1
Matthew M. Kryzanowski
Copyright © Matthew M. Kryzanowski, 2024. All Rights Reserved.
Originally Published October 2024
2nd Edition (Revised) Published May 2025
Paperback 2nd Edition (Revised) ISBN 978-1-0688629-8-4
eBook 2nd Edition (Revised) ISBN 978-1-0688629-6-0

All rights reserved. No part of this publication may be reproduced, stored or transmitted in any form or by any means, electronic, mechanical, photocopying, recording, scanning, or otherwise without written permission from the publisher. It is illegal to copy this book, post it to a website, or distribute it by any other means without permission.

Neither Idea Factory Press nor Matthew M. Kryzanowski bear responsibility for the persistence or accuracy of URLs for external or third-party Internet Websites referred to in this publication. Neither Idea Factory Press nor Matthew M. Kryzanowski guarantee that any content on such Websites is, or will remain, accurate or appropriate.

In preparation of this book for publication, best efforts for fair use and fair dealings of copyrighted material have been used by the author. If copyrighted materials have inadvertently been used without proper credit, please contact https://www.ideafactorypress.com for corrections.

Scripture quotations marked NLT are taken from the Holy Bible, New Living Translation, copyright © 1996, 2004. Used by permission of Tyndale House Publishers, Inc., Carol Stream, Illinois 60188.All rights reserved.

Scripture quotations taken from the NASB (New American Standard Bible) Copyright 1977 by The Lockman Foundation. Used by permission. All rights reserved. lockman.org

Pew Research Center bears no responsibility for the analyses or interpretations of the data presented here. The opinions expressed herein, including any implications for policy, are those of the author and not of Pew Research Center.

Idea Factory Press
https://www.ideafactorypress.com
Scarborough Canada

For My Wife, I Love You.

Contents

Acknowledgments	**11**
Introduction	**13**
Chapter 1	**25**

The Marketplace of Spiritual Ideas and the Success of Christianity   **25**
    The Protestant Reformation and the Origins of New World Christianity   25
    Toward Spiritual Freedom in the New World   28

Chapter 2   **49**

New Testament Contentions with Religious Legalism   **49**
    Acceptance of God's Law by Freedom of Conscience   49

Chapter 3   **77**

The Harms of Religious Dogma: Spiritual Gatekeeping and The Doctrine of Fear   **77**
    Preamble   77
    The Void of Being Spiritually Adrift Seeks Fulfillment   78
    Religious and Political Hierarchy Derived from Authoritarianism: A Perpetual Problem   84
    When Humanist Philosophy Tries to Resolve the Doctrine of Fear: What Happens?   87
    Psychological and Spiritual Consequences of the Doctrine of Fear   91
    Checks and Balances: Preventing Ideology Emerging from Fear Dogma   94

Chapter 4   **99**

Tension Between Predestination and Free Will: Testing Scriptural Coherence   **99**
    Message Inconsistency as a Barrier to Acceptance of Christian Faith   99
    Christian Scriptural Coherence: Examining the Bible with the Tools of Rationalism   105
    The Purpose of Entrusting Humanity to Govern the Affairs of Earth   106
    Is the Destination of the Human Soul Predetermined Whereas the Human Mind Requires Special Consideration?   107
    The Earth as the Schoolyard of Human Agency and Free Will   113

Predestination in Consideration of Heaven and Hell: On Divine Justice and Acts of Free Will in Context and Proportion   117
On the Erroneous Choice of Finite Mathematics to Measure the Infinite Love of God   120
Finding Meaning and Purpose in the Context of Predestination: Jesus Leads the Way   125
The Parable of the Vineyard Workers   128
∞ Jesus Teaches that Doing What is Right because it is the Right Thing to Do is the Work of the Christian ∞   128
What Constitutes Justice and Fairness in Fulfilling the Work of God? Contextualizing Matthew 20:15: Divine Mathematics Is Different from Human Mathematics   130
The Work of the Christian & The Wonder of Creation   131
An Alternate Proposal to Free Will ~ Determinism as a Model of Christian Existentialism: Convergence ~ Divergence Theory of Body and Spiritual Experience and Outcome   132
Conclusions: Scripture can be more Accessible by De-emphasizing Tension Between Predestination and Free Will to Change how Human ~ Divine Relations are Discussed   134

Chapter 5   139

Enter Kurt Gödel: The Limitation of Logic is that Logic is Parametric   139

Problems with Seeking Finite Logical Coherence in an Infinite Universe   139
Experimentation with the Limits of Logic in Political Discourse   148
Axiomatic Political Logic and Its Problems in Microcosm   153
Experimentation with the Limits of Logic in 'Hard' Science: Is the Universe Parametrically Bound? Or is the Universe Infinitely Expanding?   166
Systems of Logic Offer Reasonable Assurance of Certainty Through Intersubjective Agreement but are Surpassed by "Epistemological Breaks"   181
Experimentation with Limits of Moral Logic   182

Chapter 6   *189*

Anticipated Criticisms Arising and Defense of Ideas Presented   189

Defense from External Philosophical and Scientific Criticism: The Quest for Meaning is Universal Across Fields of Study   189
Defense from External Religious Criticism: Ritualism is not Analogous to Expressive and Meaningful Worship   192
Defense from Internal Christian Criticism: "Follow me, and I will make you fishers of men!" (Matthew 4:19)   195

Chapter 7   *199*

Break Free from Religious Axiom and Ritualism to Experience Spiritual Fulfillment   199

Appendix I   *207*

A Practical Proposal for the Ideologically Adrift   207
   Toward Spiritual Fulfillment by Acting Consciously in the Best Interest of Humanity (Whether the Christian Message is Accepted or Not)   207

Appendix II   211

Practical Suggestions for Church Communities   211
   Christian Spiritual Fulfillment as Conscious Practice of Free Will   211
   For Congregations: From a Church Musician's Perspective   212
   For Church Leadership (Including Musicians): Awareness of Personal Leadership Styles vs. Congregational Needs   213
   The Distinction Between Praying 'For' vs. Praying 'Upon'   214
   On the Sacraments   214
   On Trying New Ways of Doing Things   215
   Conscious Practices for Preparing for Worship   215
   For all Churchgoers   215

Works Cited   *216*

   Further Reading   221

   Glossary of Terms   225
      Historical/Political/Economic/Social Terminology   225
      Philosophical Terminology   226
      Philosophy of Mathematics Terminology   227
      Theological/Religious/Spiritual Terminology   228
      Compossibility ~ Incompossibility Theory   229
      Standard and Expanded* Use of Compossible ~ Incompossible in the Destruction of Logic from Within   229
      Theological/Religious/Spiritual Terminology Continued   229

   Supplemental Practical Material I   233

   Example of a Formal Logical Procedure   233

   Supplemental Practical Material II   235

   A Quick Glance at Kurt Gödel's Incompleteness Theorems (1931)   235
      Theorem 1   235
      Theorem 2   235

About Experiments in Christian Thought	*237*
About Idea Factory Press	*239*
About the Author	*240*
More Books by Matthew M. Kryzanowski	*241*

Acknowledgments

It is with tremendous thanks to numerous people and their direct and indirect encouragement that this book series has taken flight. First, to my brother Tim, who suggested I send an early draft of Volume 2, while it was still an essay, to various online publications simply for the sake of doing so. Tim, I owe you my gratitude for your encouragement. To Brandon, my friend and neighbor, with whom I have shared numerous deep and thoughtful conversations at school pickup and drop-off, on any number of topics of concern, including religion and spirituality, it is with great enthusiasm I look forward to many more such discussions. It was memorable, very early in the school year when you and I encountered several door-to-door evangelists on the way back from school drop-off. With them, we had a lively, intelligent, and most of all, civil conversation. To my oldest friend Ben, what is there to say? Never have I heard a discouraging word from you, and never has there been a lack of belief from you that I would do anything but excel and succeed in any pursuit or ambition that I have set out to fulfill. To my brother J, I have been greatly encouraged by your reaction to this new project of mine. Without a second thought, you immediately and enthusiastically purchased the early version of Volume 2 (before it became Volume 2). This was during the time that this undertaking was at its earliest beginning. I also enjoyed the time spent on the phone trying to explain to you what I was writing about. All of that and more has been helpful and meaningful for me. To my dad, I will say thank you for being there during difficult times, and, during countless times additionally over the years (while not always really knowing how to take my out of left-field ideas and what to do with them). Thank you for sticking it out with them nevertheless! To my Uncle Felix, it has been a wonderful experience to connect and to find common interests while undertaking this project. Thank you for your generosity by agreeing to take the time to painstakingly proofread the first edition of this volume. Thank you as well for making helpful suggestions and asking some challenging questions (they are my favorite kind). To Aunt Jane as well, I wish you and Uncle Felix all the best in your spiritually innovative endeavors. RCWP Canada is exactly the kind of spiritual organization that encourages independent and critical thinking with all things pertaining to religious practice. That questions of theology matter are in the way they urge people seeking to maintain established and uncontested religious doctrine uncomfortable. In this, questions of theology are something of invaluable importance. I am encouraged and inspired by your work. To Vicar Noah at Hope Evangelical Lutheran Church in Toronto, you are a man of great conviction and of good heart. May you cease not to teach and preach. Additionally, may you continue to lead people through difficult times by your great example. To Rev. John Brown, Rev. T. Leigh Olson, to the choir, and to all the people at Church of the Master United Church in Scarborough (now disbanded), thank you for helping me to set sail on my own spiritual journey. You have indirectly helped me to weather the current storm I have found myself to be in, in ways you do not know. To my mom, what can I really say? I mean along with pop, you continue to encourage me without fail, even when my ideas continue to arrive from left field. I am happy to feel encouraged in perpetuity to keep doing my thing. Although, I have not yet won seven super bowl rings (ha ha) you know what I am talking about. To my daughters, thank you for taking up the torch (by osmosis mostly) of not accepting things at face value, and for continuing the family business of having innate curiosity and of questioning everything. May it serve you well. To Beth, John, and Robbie, thanks for being there during these otherworldly times. If there is anyone else who I have forgotten to include, I'm sure I will think of you about 7 seconds after I click 'Publish Book'. To you as well, thank you. Finally, For my wife Jen, my sweetie, my love, yes, your knight in shining (rusting) armor still looks a lot like an idiot in tinfoil despite his best intentions. I'm sure he will continue to stand in the outfield and scratch his head. Although, this time, he will likely be thinking about the tinfoil itself, and how it could generate enough solar power to keep the electricity that will always be there alive and well. In that regard, the Gil Blas part of me that led me to Toronto and to you has morphed into more of a Don Quixote.

Jen

I love you and always will,

Matt

February 4th, 2025

The Destruction of Logic from Within

Introduction

The limits of logic in the pursuit of a deeper understanding of the nature of reality have been met by philosophers, mathematicians, scientists, theologians, psychologists, and by people from any field of study, or walk of life, no matter their religious, political, of any intellectual affiliation or belief. Any curious and thinking person who engages with abstract thought, the material world, or the nature of the cosmos, will inevitably run up against limitations of the ability for reason and logic, and additionally for scientific observation and method, to explain, to interact with, and to understand the mysteries of the universe.

To offer a fresh perspective on the nature and limits of logic as the most appealed to way of understanding and experiencing the natural world and the nature of reality, this book will apply the lens of 'the incompossible' to the accepted and often reflexively assumed viewpoint that logic, systems of logic, and procedures of logical operations alone are the source of what constitutes truth. This book will also question the assumption that what solely forms and substantiates properties and principles of physical reality as 'truth', and even stand-alone (declarative) 'truth' cannot be fully understood by the human mind in the absence of an external point of reference. It will be argued that the breakdown of logical reasoning occurs most often when 'truth' is expressed solely as an axiom (a fixed object or material, a declarative idea, or a statement, or a compelled or even voluntary ritual, or act of will). When such 'truisms' become operative in the process of their fulfillment and completion, it will be shown that logic, as a finite tool of understanding, is limited in its ability to help people to fully comprehend what is an infinite and immeasurable universe. This being because no person can possess all-knowingness. It will be argued therefore that people will benefit from turning to alternate channels of thought to understand the nature and reality of the universe and to know God fully and more deeply.

In philosophical and theological usage, 'incompossible' is a term that has been used to describe ideas and substances that contain properties of internal contradiction and properties too much in contradiction to other substances and ideas in creation, and as such, they are not chosen by God for creation. Therefore, they are not part of the created world. In times since the term came into standard philosophical usage, philosophers have proposed that incompossible ideas and substances are tools available to God to use in His creation. Although incompossible ideas and substance are conceivable, it has been argued (particularly by Gottfried Wilhelm Leibniz), that God does not choose to create the universe from incompossible constructs. God does not choose from incompossible ideas and substance, it has been historically argued because incompossible constructs are of such inadequate quality that they are incompatible with the goodness of His creation. The term was brought into standard philosophical usage by Gottfried Wilhelm Leibniz (1646-1716). G.W. Leibniz was a German Enlightenment Mathematician and a Philosopher as well. Although there are examples of usage of the term 'incompossibility', and its inversion: 'compossibility', prior to G.W. Leibniz's deployment of it, it is Leibniz who is most often associated with bringing these concepts into philosophical and even theological prominence.

From the definition of the term 'incompossible', then the term 'compossible', it is accurate to infer, refers to ideas and substances that are of optimal quality, such that they are not internally contradictory in any way. As such, compossible ideas and substances are highly compatible with, and not in any way contradictory to the rest of God's creation, and its goodness. Therefore, God has chosen from compossible things to be used exclusively for the goodness of His creation. Compossible ideas and substances as universal constructs are therefore thought to have no internally contradictory properties, and to contain no properties that are in contradiction with the created universe. It ought to be pointed out as well that under the theory of compossibility of creation, there are many things that are conceivably compossible, yet some of these things, that although they are compossible, are not of the highest and most optimal of compossible quality and therefore are not chosen from to form the created universe. This point has been part of the line of reasoning and the argument for compossibility theory during its history as well.

The terminology of compossible ~ incompossible as a model for explaining the metaphysics of creation will be adapted and loosened for the purposes of this book. The usage in this book of the compossible ~ incompossible paradigm as a description of metaphysical duality as a model for creation will still retain its philosophical and theological character. However, the terminology will be deployed from time to time in a more flexible way to describe acts of free will carried out by human beings, which might be either compatible with or incompatible with God's creation and its goodness, or it might be used additionally to describe acts of free will, that cause degradation to the compossible quality of existence. Further, the compossible ~ incompossible model for understanding the created world will be used as a tool of analysis for seemingly paradoxical concepts and points of contention found in the Christian message itself. When used in this way, the compossible ~ incompossible duality will be applied to clarify points of perceived incoherence in biblical scripture where there is thought to be internal contradiction, and where seeming biblical contradiction is viewed as a barrier to accepting the Christian message as a result.

By proposing that logic is a limited tool of thought, and yet, that it might paradoxically contain within it the ability to be surpassed by its own limitations, is not meant to say that logic itself is incompossible with the goodness of creation, nor is it even to say that the tools of logic and reason are without importance (they are extremely important for the human capacity to continue to thrive). But rather, it is to say that just as biblical scripture is thought to have internal contradiction, logic, and its affiliated toolkit of activities, as a way of understanding truth, can reach a point of internal breakdown and incoherence similarly.

By proposing the idea that internal breakdown and destabilization of logic, even though logic is a wonderful tool of advancing human understanding, it will be argued that breakdown and destabilization of logic, is itself logically useful for people to achieve greater understanding and greater awareness of the nature of reality. Breakdown and destabilization of logic suggests that from within it, there lies an opportunity for spiritual growth, and even reason to accept the assurance of God's limitless goodness, immeasurable love, and unattainable wisdom as a sensible decision. This acceptance being in acknowledgement and understanding that human knowledge and wisdom is limited greatly in its scope and capacity.

If the limits of logical knowing are understood this way, the rationalist, the agnostic, the atheist, the spiritually questioning, and otherwise inclined persons, will have a strengthened understanding of the Christian pathway to greater spiritual awareness, and to know the human place and purpose in a universe created for the good. It is through conscious understanding and rational acceptance of finite human limitations, the suggestion will be made, that freely choosing a personal spiritual relationship with

God offers people optimal opportunity to transcend the physical experience of human misery, suffering and death.

The book builds on itself chapter by chapter. Chapter One contains a brief history of religious persecution in pre-Enlightenment Europe. It will tell the story of the consequent influx to North America of people with deeply held religious convictions beginning around the time of the Protestant Reformation. This mass departure from Europe brought to the New World the idea and spirit of freedom of thought and freedom of expression as desirable as guiding standards for ethics and morality (even if, at times, the realization of such ideals has fallen short and continues to fall short). With relevance to this volume, this fresh kind of individualism, and its influence on New World religious and spiritual life and belief, will be shown to have been and will continue to be of benefit. The benefit being because of the emphasis placed on personal responsibility for spiritual development and growth in this way of thinking, rather than spiritual development being imposed on the individual by way of adherence to customary religious cultural tradition, or through adherence to prescribed religious societal norms for their own sake.

Chapters Two and Three will discuss the problems that can arise from human-made codification of religious doctrine. These chapters will expose the problems with, and the spiritual limitations of excessive adherence to strict religious customary law, and they will highlight the kinds of problems that can arise with the over-ritualization of spiritual practices. From a scriptural and philosophical perspective, it will be argued that these kinds of faulty constructs act as an encumbrance to the pursuit of free spiritual awareness and experience. This will be examined in the Christian sense and briefly touched upon in a more general way with respect to religious traditions and their uncomfortable conflations with political experiences throughout history and into present times.

For the rationalist skeptic, Chapter Four will put the scripture of the Christian Faith under scrutiny for its logical coherence. A seeming internal contradiction arises in the Bible from the New Testament by its insistence that Jesus offers humanity the choice to freely accept God and His love, and additionally that Jesus' message for humanity to do right by each other through freedom of conscience reflects God's image back to him, is seemingly in contradiction to the opposing view (also quite easily to be inferred from Christian scripture), that human life is predetermined in all its facets. The final logical extension of proposed Bible-based absolute determinism is of course, that the decision as to who will be predestined to enter Heaven has already been made. It will be shown that subscribers to this type of doctrine premise their belief on guesswork. The pre-determinist holds that because God has all knowledge of the past, present, and future, and is at the same time an all-powerful and supreme being. Yet, this is a problem of seeming inconsistency in the document that many Christians consider to be the inerrant, infallible, or even 'merely' the inspired word of God. The theological problem of predestination vs. free will in Christian scripture will be taken apart and analyzed to assess its validity. Something of a proposed settlement to the contention toward this seemingly incoherent biblical messaging will be offered. For some clarity, Chapter Four will seek to provide a fresh perspective regarding the tension that free will and predestination exhibit in the study of Christian scripture. Chapter Four will show how such seeming paradoxes are more often problems of limited human understanding, but can be useful to reflect on, to deepen individual spiritual awareness and understanding, and to help provide an improved sense of internal personal contentment, and fulfillment.

Chapter Five forms the focal point of the book. In this part, the idea that axiomatic logic and formal methods of logical process are thought to contain universal properties of truth, or that they can solely and fully reveal what is universally 'true', will be put under scrutiny for logical coherence and internal contradiction. Kurt Gödel's Incompleteness Theorems (1931) will be deployed for this purpose by way of using them for thought experimentation from the perspective of various domains of human understanding. This will be done to show the nature of universal 'truth' is undecidable when approached solely by way of logical understanding.

The idea of 'truth as (unqualified) axiom' will be shown to be a faulty concept in the absence of a point of reference. It will also hopefully be demonstrated that formal logic as a methodical process is finite (by its own definition), therefore containing limitations, and will thus, break down under the weight of its own parameters. This will be shown to occur particularly when undecidability is inserted into the parametric binding of a 'closed loop' set of axioms. Logical axiom, logical scientific processes and logical formalism of procedure can very often create a reasonable degree of assurance that there is universal 'certainty', and this will be shown to be sound reasoning in the replicability of such procedures. Yet, it will be argued that these powerful and successful tools of the rational human mind cannot on their own provide fully or completely, understanding of the unimaginably immense and infinite universe, or can such limited human capacity answer for the why of its existence.

Jesus' unprecedented upset to the existing pre-Messianic dogmatic concepts of God's law, religious legalism, and beliefs about how to make oneself acceptable in the eyes of God, will be viewed as the infusion of the 'Paradox of Undecidability' into the Mediterranean understanding of human ethics, morality, and the nature of God. The definition of the Paradox of Undecidability, as it will be further described below, will be shown to be very much compatible with Jesus' message to humanity by his dismantlement and overturning of previously held 'truths' about the nature of God. By being thought of this way, the life, teachings, death, and resurrection of Jesus Christ can be seen as an act of God willing the incompossible as an infusion of contradiction into the His world, created from compossible ideas. By choosing to will the incompossible into His own compossible creation, God demonstrated that by inserting an undecidability of belief into the physical laws of His created world, breaking free from habits of customary and axiomatic religious 'truisms' and ritualism, is therefore much more important when compassion calls for it, than it is to adhere to such laws of logical 'truism' for their own sake, and when it results in ignoring the humanity in others. The spiritually seeking individual will hopefully find this proposition will open their mind to the perspective that God's love for His creation is abundant, limitless in power and incalculable in its wisdom, when God as Truth is understood not wholly from a logical perspective.

Regarding the tremendous historical significance of Kurt Gödel's Incompleteness Theorems (1931) and drawn from within them the Paradox of Undecidability (demonstrated to be found in the idea of mathematical logical incoherence), Gödel's Incompleteness Theorems caused a rethink of the notion of mathematical certainty. Even though mathematics and mathematical philosophy are very much foundational to human thought and understanding (and even foundational to the very success and prosperity of humanity), the upheaval and turmoil his theorems created spilled over into the realm of philosophical reasoning as well.

Historically, the most demonstrative example of the impact that Gödel's work had, and that which best characterizes the impact the Incompleteness Theorems have had on the development of modern logic, is in the upset they caused to the painstaking work of Bertrand Russell (1872-1970) and of Alfred North Whitehead (1861-1947) in their three-volume work Principia Mathematica (1910).

Bertrand Russell and Alfred North Whitehead had attempted to thoroughly validate, and at the same time, sought as best as possible to clarify and to strengthen the connection between mathematics and logical reasoning. Their efforts included at least trying to minimize the use of axiom as truth in mathematical theory. To do so, they attempted to streamline and simplify the use of ordered sets of symbols as tools of representation for ideas to help to resolve the problems of paradox that were already being called into question in mathematics before Gödel had done so.

With mathematics being a field of study primed for the use of symbols of representation as a form of axiomatic thought, and also, with its reliance on the use of ordered sets like ordinal numbers for example, as an area foundational to human knowledge and wisdom, mathematics was and is very much embedded with symbols as axioms of 'truth'. That symbols and the ordering of symbols into sets are tools and operations of mathematics were and are often very much presupposed to contain certain properties of elemental 'truth'. This is often the case without challenge to the very premise that symbols do represent truth, that they can be guaranteed to contain and to uphold properties of certainty within them, or that even in the manipulation of such symbols and sets, that such operations can create or even enable something of further meaning within the properties of the symbols of mathematics. The Russell-Whitehead work had recognized these problems, yet did not meet its objective to rectify them. In the mathematical crisis that was beginning to manifest in what was and still is an established pillar of foundational human knowledge and wisdom, the early 20th century effort by Russell and Whitehead, to create Principia Mathematica ultimately succumbed to logical incoherence and was rendered discreditable by the problem of mathematical undecidability under the Gödel Theorems. This was despite Russell and Whitehead's best efforts to provide assurance of logical constancy in mathematics.

Chapter Five, as with the rest of the book, serves as a form of Christian apologetics. To uphold the strength and the immeasurable value of the Christian message in ways that would hopefully appeal to rational skeptics, it is hoped that the reader will come to view the impact the Incompleteness Theorems have had on rationalism and logic, as the go-to source of knowledge and wisdom, long unchallenged as a way for people to agree as to what is truth, particularly in modern Western civilization. In this, it is hoped that the reader will seek to at least minimally breach their own limits of personal logical understanding and find an opportunity to seek spiritual awareness, development, knowledge, and fulfillment.

By overlaying Kurt Gödel's work (that had the effect of destabilizing human intellectual foundations), with the normal, and additionally, more expanded and more flexible philosophical and theological usage of Gottfried Wilhelm Leibniz's compossibility ~ incompossibility theory of God's infinite creative abilities, it is intended that this book will provide the reader with a gateway to Christian thought as an opportunity for spiritual development and growth. It is hoped the familiar ways of accepting Christian Faith will be defended and upheld similarly through expressing them from what may be seen as a fresh perspective.

In doing so, this offering will seek to demonstrate that rationalism is not incompatible with spirituality, but rather, can enjoy a complementary relationship in the human psyche. Readers of any background, religious affiliation, or spiritual inclination may hopefully find this work appealing to their mindset.

Chapter Six defends the concepts in this book against anticipated criticism that may arise. This part will include defense from points of perceived inaccuracy in the interpretation of Christian scripture and consequent exegetical standards as a result. As well, religious, spiritual, and theological criticism external to Christian theology and belief will be addressed, as will expected rationalist philosophical and scientific criticisms that might arise from the challenges and discomfort this volume might present to people who strictly permit their faith to reside in scientific method and logical formalism.

Chapter Seven provides something of a conclusion and the Appendices are more practical in nature and provide uses for the ideas presented in this volume. These might or might not be applicable to a range of individuals from various backgrounds and walks of life.

Chapter 1

The Marketplace of Spiritual Ideas and the Success of Christianity

The Protestant Reformation and the Origins of New World Christianity

Why do Christian activities generally thrive more in the United States while they are in greater decline in other parts of the Western World? The success of Christianity in the United States is thanks to the idea of openness and exchange that since colonial times, the settlers who arrived seeking a better life for themselves brought with them.

While many colonists came from Europe to the North American continent seeking their fortune, many people who came were misunderstood, or worse, perceived as a threat to pre-established order in their country of origin. The latter often departed under duress, fleeing Europe under the threat of persecution on religious grounds. From at least as early as the 17th century onward if not earlier, Christians from Protestant and certain Catholic backgrounds alike fled from various corners of Europe under threat of violence and death, to practice their religious beliefs as they felt their conscience guided them to do (Seymour, 1997, pp. 19-20).

With the prior development of the printing press, improvements in literacy rates, and the proliferation of religious materials across Europe during this period, it was becoming clear to those holding power in monarchical Europe that attempts to uphold the religious hierarchies embedded into society were beginning to falter (Chadwick, 1988, p. 24).

One of the ways those who were holding absolutist power responded to social upheaval resulting from the transition of Europe from the age of Absolutism toward what became the European Enlightenment was by the enforcement of social cohesion. Religion was of much greater consideration to people at that time than in Europe today. As such, for monarchies to enforce social cohesion, to uphold existing European hierarchies of governance, the lever of religious persecution was deployed as a tool of coercion (Chadwick, 1988, pp. 125, 153, 365).

The age of Absolutism in Europe was struggling to survive, and the era of Enlightenment was emerging. By insisting that people deemed to be religiously nonconformist or religious dissenters must adhere to customary religious, and societal norms, and laws regarding religion imposed by monarchy, or face persecution and death otherwise, the age of absolute monarchical power was grasping to maintain supreme authority over society.

Progress made in the realms of philosophical, economic, and scientific areas of study, and additionally, improvements and advancements made in understanding of any number of intellectual activities and enterprises, meant that the intellectual progress being created began to lead to tangible improvements in the material conditions of ordinary people (Chadwick, 1988, pp. 29-30). For spiritually minded people, the benefit of this transitional period in European history was an abundance of religious literary materials that were becoming available to the individual person (Chadwick, 1988, p. 29).

Thus, to keep people of lower standing in check, it became more difficult for monarchists, and the church as complicit in attempting to uphold state authority, to maintain a grasp on religious narratives as a form of gatekeeping. For example, it was becoming questionable as to why it was necessary to hear the Gospel spoken solely in Liturgical Latin, given that the language of scholarship in other fields was beginning to shift toward the vernacular (Chadwick, 1988, pp. 298-299). That a person could hear the Gospel and even read it in one's own language meant that scripture was demystified, more relatable, and less in need of a clerical intermediary for its interpretation. The effect of these societal shifts became one of destabilization of the Roman Catholic Church's authority on matters and affairs governing eternal well-being for individual people.

At the time, there were influential figures who had begun to pop up around Europe and were questioning Roman Catholic doctrine. Among them, Ulrich Zwingli (1484-1531) of Switzerland, John Calvin (1509-1564) of France, Jacques Lefèvre (1450-1536) of France, William Tyndale (c.1490-1536) of England, and Patrick Hamilton (1504-1528) of Scotland. Additionally, the merchants of the Hanseatic League brought the idea of religious reformation to the northern reaches of Europe to Scandinavia during their commercial travels and affairs (Dunstan, 1961, pp. 15-22).

The movement toward religious reform in this era was likely somewhat a decentralized and organic process, although reformers began to influence each other and discover their commonalities in thinking. Perhaps among the most well-known and influential figures of the Protestant Reformation was Martin Luther (1483-1586) of Germany.

Martin Luther was ordained to the Catholic Church in 1507, despite his many misgivings about problems with Church doctrine. Between 1517-1522, by his own choice, Martin Luther was motivated by his contempt for Church practices and was moved to harshly and outwardly criticize the Roman Catholic Church. He had composed the Ninety-Five Theses (1517), in which he was quite brazenly critical of Catholic Church administration, arguing that many of the elements of Church affairs coming into practice (indulgences) were rife with abuse, and were being used as a tool for personal gain by those seeking influence within the Church (Walker, 1970, pp. 302-305).

Originally composed in Latin, Luther sent his Ninety-Five Theses in a letter to the Archbishop of Mainz, and as well, posted copies on the doors of various churches around Wittenberg Germany on All Saints Day in 1517. In this act of provocation, the Protestant Reformation continued to gain further influence (Walker, 1970, p. 305).

An unacceptable concept to church authorities preceding this time, the movement toward individual spirituality, to be able to bypass the priesthood as intermediary between the individual and God was becoming an acceptable viewpoint and practice. It was becoming not only possible, but acceptable for the average person to dare to reflect freely upon matters pertaining to their personal spiritual well-being, and to question Roman Catholic interpretation of scripture and practices.

For Protestant groups across Europe, the belief that it was scripture itself that was the source of Christian authority and not the Church and its governance structure, was becoming an entrenched and acceptable belief (Reese, 1999, p. 614).

Toward Spiritual Freedom in the New World

In the Ninety-Five Theses, Martin Luther had outlined that the Catholic Church was offering false salvation in many of its practices. Luther came to be seen as a threat to established religious hierarchy and order, among those who were named above, and others additionally, by making things uncomfortable for Catholic Church authorities. Luther and others were actively calling into question the supreme authority the Catholic Church had claimed for itself over many centuries, on matters of spiritual and religious affairs (Walker, 1970, pp. 312-316).

The spirit of the Protestant Reformation was not one of questioning God or even calling the existence of God into question. Although Humanism as a philosophical school of thought associated with Desiderius Erasmus (1467-1536), had begun developing before the Protestant Reformation had begun to emerge (Reese, 1999, p. 316). Humanism borne from the Renaissance period was different in many ways from Humanism in present times. Humanism in the Renaissance did not mean that the development of human morality was possible, or even necessarily desirable in the absence of God, but rather, the Humanism of the Renaissance was one of returning to traditional forms of Greek logic and inquiry (Reese, 1999, pp. 316-317). The Humanist movement therefore was very much in support of the spirit of the Reformation in the sense of moving toward genuine permissibility to question church authorities on matters of scriptural interpretation (Reese, 1999, pp. 316-317).

For it to have been proposed that individual people could be marginally competent enough, or intellectually capable enough to bypass religious intermediaries as solely specialized interpreters of Christian scripture, and to advocate for the formation of a personal relationship with God, marked a revolutionary shift in spiritual and religious thinking in Christian life. This type of revolutionary shift was what made the Protestant Reformation radically distinct from previous reformations, councils, and schisms within the Church, and this distinguishing feature is what made the Protestant Reformation the existential threat to the Catholic Church that it was.

The possibility of new ways of relating to God gained traction across Europe at a speed with which the Roman Catholic Church was woefully unprepared. Given human nature, unsurprisingly, the shift resulted in tremendous amounts of bloodshed by way of conflict, revolt, uprisings, and even all-out war. Violence resulted while the spiritual and religious mindset and landscape across Europe was dramatically transformed during the Protestant Reformation.

By 1648, the European continent was turning out to be religiously divided from top to bottom. The northern portions of Europe tilted toward Protestantism, while the southern regions of Europe were maintaining their Catholic religious character. Yet, at this time, many states were still unresolved in their spiritual and religious leanings amidst the turmoil and upset (Chadwick, 1988, p. 366).

Because many Europeans were beginning to put into practice the idea that they were free to contemplate things pertaining to their personal salvation, to eternal life, and to the nature and understanding of God, this resulted in the development of new ways of practicing Christianity in the centuries following the Reformation. The shift had resulted in the emergence of new branches of Christian practice, and of religious organization, with various reinterpretations, and as well, new interpretations of the Holy Bible. The creation of newly translated versions of the Bible into the vernacular were published, and new ideas about how to live by reinterpreted or newly created religious doctrine derived from scripture, was all put into the efforts of spiritual and religious concern. This brought about freshly determined opinions and practices as to how spiritual life ought to be lived and fulfilled. Like-minded groups and individuals found each other and began to organize and adopt various similar practices, making them distinct organizations from other religious groups.

In response to state-supported persecution of people in European nations who refused to adhere to, or comply with their state-backed religious doctrine, many people decided to seek out the shores of the New World. Many people departed from numerous parts of Europe to carry out and to practice deeply held spiritual and religious beliefs and convictions in the New World. This included people from both Catholic and Protestant groups alike.

Without offering an opinion about the merits and/or problems with various belief systems and/or practices of various religious groups who left Europe for North America, among the Christian groups who arrived first onto the shores of the New World included a settlement of English Protestants known as Puritans who were critical of Anglicanism and Catholicism and was largely disenfranchised with religious life in England. They arrived in North America as early as 1630. Once again, without necessity to offer an opinion about the various kinds of spiritual and religious practices and beliefs held by arriving groups of Christians, the Puritans were eventually joined by Mennonites, Huguenots, Jesuits, Lutherans, Irish Catholics, Congregationalists, Calvinists, Baptists, as well as other groups who might have come to voluntarily seek improved spiritual opportunity. Many religious groups additionally came from Europe with the prospect to spread their beliefs among people who had not yet heard the gospel across the Atlantic that were becoming newly known to Europeans. As well, religious people and groups who came to North America might have initially been in 'good standing' (so to speak) within their country of origin but eventually came to be viewed as 'non-conforming' Christian believers within their home country. Nevertheless, the process of exiting Europe for the shores of the New World can be thought of as something of an emptying of spiritually and religious minded people from Europe during this phase of the Reformation. Yet, the spiritual emptying, reordering of society, and the political restructuring that Europe was experiencing marked something of an expression of newfound spiritual transformation across the Atlantic Ocean (https://www.loc.gov/exhibits/religion/index.html, 2024).

After the precedent of seeking out the shores of North America was established, during subsequent centuries, people with broad ranges of religious conscience and belief gradually and continually left many regions of Europe. Eventually, people from other parts of the world who were persecuted for their religious and spiritual practices came to North America as well. Often, they too came seeking freedom from religious persecution and duress, and the freedom to practice and profess their spiritual and religious beliefs undisturbed similarly, and without fear of reprisal (https://www.loc.gov/exhibits/religion/index.html, 2024).

It was strongly debated as to what degree religion should play in the character of the colonies, and in the development of the United States as an independent nation. Yet, the aspiration toward a society built on freedom of conscience was becoming accepted on its merits as a way for the newly emerging nation to manage its affairs (Seymour, 1997, p. 20).

It should be noted that during the transition to the period of European Enlightenment following from the Protestant Reformation, that although most often through resolution by brutality and bloodshed, Protestantism as a valid Christian practice gradually came to be normalized, accepted, or at least was conceded by European systems of governance to be valid religious practice in many nation-states. Although this turned out to be the case, many Europeans continued to depart for the New World for reasons of improved spiritual and economic prospects well into the 19th century, while the conflation between state and religion continued to co-mingle and to remain intertwined in Europe (Seymour, 1997, pp. 19-21).

The claim to improvements in spiritual well-being, along with improvements to material well-being in the United States from the early 19th century up to the early 20th centuries have been documented in the observations and research carried out by German Sociologist (and the person considered to be the founder of modern social sciences), Max Weber (1864-1920) in his work: The Protestant Ethic and the Spirit of Capitalism (1905).

Based on Weber's travel to the United States in 1904, and from his recorded observations and research, which were a result of his time and effort there, Weber produced his 'Social Science' treatise in which he drew conclusions attributing the rise in material prosperity in the United States in large part to what he described as the 'Protestant Ethic'. It should be noted however, that direct credit of a 'Protestant Ethic' as being the sole source of rising American prosperity is very much a topic in dispute (Harrington, 1987, pp. 240-241). Also, it should be noted that the 'methodology' Weber used in carrying out his research would have of course not have been to modern standards, given that the field of Social Science was newly emerging. Weber's research methods and observations were in contention even shortly after his work was published. For further discussion and analysis near-contemporary to Weber's time, please see: (Green, 1959).

Yet, even prior to Weber's observations and research, early French Sociologist and Journalist, Alexis de Tocqueville (1805-1859) produced a two-volume work: Democracy in America (1835-1840), in which de Tocqueville outlined similar observations upon visit to the United States. De Tocqueville's observations were comparable to Weber's in that they connected rising material prosperity with the democratic ethos, and the benefit of self-autonomy of individual to manage personal affairs with free market idealism. De Tocqueville's experience in the United States, and his observations, were very much compatible with Weber's perspective. Included in this was the way that de Tocqueville had related the benefits the young nation was experiencing, both in social and economic spheres, from having chosen to decouple the unpleasantries that arise when religious experience is tied up with government matters, and when government matters are tied into religious experience (Tocqueville, 2004 pg. 666-668).

In present times, upon returning to Europe to report their findings (as social scientists), both de Tocqueville and Weber would undoubtedly be considered to have used flawed research methodology, and as well, would be considered to have used inconsistent methods of reporting their findings, and would be seen as perhaps unaware of cognitive biases they might have been confirming from within their own preconceptions. Additionally, they would likely be viewed as being unaware of other skewed cognitive biases through which they may have been observing and experiencing life in the United States. Nevertheless, upon carrying out their efforts, and upon completing their work, de Tocqueville and Weber both created invaluable first-hand documentation of early 19th century through to early 20th century American life. As such, positive conclusions can be drawn from their efforts to record and present the success of the American model of government, and the American way of life to their fellow Europeans upon their return. De Tocqueville's work had additionally researched farther back to the origins of American ideals, but again, to be taken for what it is and what it is not.

What the work of both men showed to scholars and other interested parties upon returning to the European was that correlations existed among democratic ideals, freedom to pursue personal interests, the ideal of physical material marketplaces, commercial marketplaces, and by extension, the benefit of having a relaxed marketplace of ideas, resulting in improved well-being both spiritually and economically for Americans. The conclusion that minimal interference from government in commercial activities, and in personal and spiritual affairs by the levers of governmental authority, can be drawn from both Weber and de Tocqueville's work. What Weber's and de Tocqueville's observations of the situation in the United

States during that era in the American story offer is an affirmation that merit-based approaches toward attaining societal prosperity and well-being (personal, spiritual, and material) is indeed credible, but more-so, it can even be a desirable foundation upon which to build a prosperous and healthy civilization.

With respect to divergence in religious and spiritual practices from the European tradition, where the mixing of politics with religion resulted in unpredictable and negative outcomes for individuals and society, it was during the development of the American Constitution that attempts for any sort of formation of a national religious system to become established and maintained by and through government channels was ultimately ineffectual (Seymour, 1997, p. 54). As early as the time of the American Revolution, the desire for ways of doing things British or continental European was being viewed with skepticism and being rejected by design in the United States. However, the interplay between religion and state was a hotly debated point of controversy before and during those times, and it remains very much a point of heated contention and source of disagreement in American political discourse to this day. For a more comprehensive viewpoint on that matter please see: (Wills, 2008).

Between 1787-1789, the Constitution of the United States of America was drawn up, ratified, and put into place as irrefutable law. In it, there was no pretense that religious custom of any sort must be adhered to, nor would any such custom be imposed onto the citizenry, in any way, by the Government of the United States of America. Whether freedom from such an encumbrance has been characterized as governmental indifference to religious affairs (Wills, 2008, p. 234), or, if it has been viewed as a move toward aspirational ideal, the development of the First Amendment in the Bill of Rights has had a central role in shaping the spiritual and religious character of the United States of

America. The First Amendment of the Bill of Rights contained in the United States Constitution states:

"Congress shall make no law respecting an establishment of religion, or prohibiting the free exercise thereof; or abridging the freedom of speech, or of the press; or the right of the people peaceably to assemble, and to petition the Government for a redress of grievances."

Sourced from: (The Constitution: A Collection of Historically Important Communications of the United States of America. 1776-1963, 2014, p. 31)

Through the ratification of the Constitution (1788), and the ratification of the Bill of Rights (1791), the development and ratification of American law in its formation has made it clear that the European way was not the will of the American. Again, whether through indifference to personal religious, spiritual, and economic life, or whether it has been through encouragement of individual aspiration, the United States of America, from its outset, has become known as the land of freedom of conscience, the land of freedom of expression, and the land of freedom to pursue one's own way of life as one sees fit. In much the same way that the Protestant Reformation brought about a spiritual transformation in Europe, it was clear that the way in which the United States sought to conduct its political affairs was transformational in its newness of approach, and in the optimism of its outlook (Seymour, 1997, p. 20).

Even if it has not necessarily always been carried out with its best possible use, or its best possible implementation after its creation, it remains true to present times that the Constitution of the United States excuses the American citizenry from the burdensome pretense of interference and meddling from governmental authority on matters pertaining to personal religious and spiritual affairs. Perhaps still to a high degree, yet perhaps to a much lesser extent than in the past, arguably, the economic and social aspects of American life remain possible to be carried on within the United States, without necessity for concern of government interference for its citizenry into the present time. The United States and its model of government remains among the most successful in that regard. What is clear from the founding documents, is that under the American structure of government, the concept of nation was one built on the premise that government was there to facilitate the interests of the people, and not the other way around.

In contrast to the way procedural functions of European parliamentary democracies are carried out, the American model of hands-off governance by premise likely will not and does not as easily result in state-endorsed mandates to seek to optimize societal or individual outcomes. Whether this results in better or worse collective or individualized outcomes for society, or even whether it matters, can be a quite heated discussion point as well as religious matters. However, by having freedom at least by aspirational premise to pursue personal ambitions and interests (that can be pursued in spite of government efforts that might present obstruction, or that might seek to extract from the personally successful to fund questionable government-supported projects), the autonomy of the individual, and the responsibility of the individual to seek to create the outcome they desire for themselves, and for their family (spiritually or otherwise), is notable in the American mindset and in American society (Seymour, 1997, p. 19). The degree to which individual personal responsibility is something of an important and tremendous undertaking, both in its prospect for abundant success, and in the specter of grim failure as possibility, the idea of being able to start over forms a significant feature of the American psyche in the cultural narrative of 'redemption' from personal economic failure, and the promise of starting over 'rebirth', held in American society. Matters of opportunity and outcome in the United States continue to be a source of inspiration for sparking questions, concerns, and debate regarding the degree to which individuals and/or government ought to be responsible for, or ought to care for their struggling neighbor during difficult economic times.

Gains made in American prosperity by having a 'hands-off' government were, as observed by de Tocqueville and Weber, seen in most aspects of American society, including, agriculture, commerce, technology, science, literature, art, medicine, intellectual, artistic, and various spiritual pursuits, including developments in matters of faith and religion. For further reading and analysis regarding the development of American prosperity and well-being, particularly during the 19th and 20th centuries, please see: (Gordon, 2016), (Greenspan & Wooldridge, 2018), (Kirk, 1992), and (Seymour, 1997).

That there are benefits or drawbacks to a merit based free-market economy of goods, services, and ideas remains a point of lively discussion, debate, and contention in present times, as mentioned previously. In the present time additionally, discussion on these matters is often very likely underwritten by political interest groups and well-funded organizations supporting and bolstering their own political agendas. Nonetheless, the United States of America has been demonstrated to be a world-leader in material and economic innovation, boosting prosperity and in improved health and well-being on many fronts, for much of its existence. Notably, this has been achieved despite an indifference to or lack of assurance of individual outcome from government. The shouldering of personal responsibility directly onto the individual in the United States is quite disproportionate when viewed in contrast to promises made by many nation-states likewise industrialized, yet, perhaps more responsible through the design of their government structure and development of policy, to require greater collective responsibility ('facilitated' by government), for assurance of individual well-being and outcome. As a point of consideration and contrast, many improvements to the standard of living for Americans from the laissez-faire model of commerce from late 19th century to the late 20th century are argued to have been unprecedented, and as such, not likely repeatable as to the level of prosperity created by such innovations going forward (Gordon, 2016, p. 17).

After accounting for matters of material improvement and higher standards of material well-being contrasted by the European standard of living in the 19th and early 20th century, it should be noted that matters of spiritual well-being in decline in the United States have followed a similar trajectory as Europe toward the end of the 20th century and into the 21st century, but to a lesser extent. Nonetheless, with an abundance of material prosperity created by Americans historically, Americans have given serious consideration to, and have consistently sought out, and found innovative ways to help fulfill the need for spiritual nourishment in American society and beyond. It has been individual citizens and self-organized community efforts of Americans themselves that have historically led the way to meet the spiritual needs of fellow citizens and the needs of nations lagging in prosperity and health. This corresponds to with rising economic success of built from the American way of life.

In the American model of government and its premise of facilitating economic opportunity, and additionally, in the open avenues of exploration created by Americans to seek personal growth through spiritual fulfillment, by way of self-directed interest and personal responsibility, Americans have more than risen to the occasion and to meet needs in this regard. While it might be viewed as a tremendous belief in, and respect implied for the capability of the individual citizen to manage his or her own spiritual and religious affairs (and to decide what is best for particular familial considerations), or whether by contrastive perspective, there is implied indifference to the same, it is notable that, for example, religious self-organization and community spiritual group efforts have encouraged the assurance of a reasonable prospect of positive outcome for fellow citizens, and concern for their well-being. This is notable as well because such generosity often occurs in the absence of, or even despite built-in structures of government bureaucracy, and various levers and layers of government power and authority that might be a source of obstruction, or of unnecessary competition (whether they might be of an inadvertent nature or an intentional one) Please see: (Ferguson, 2014) for more about the problem of government overreach correlating with the erosion of civic responsibilities.

In most facets of life, the way of the New World was, and has become, a jarring, yet positive departure from the European way of doing things. The societal benefits have been very much thanks to built-in consideration for intentional relaxation of government influence and overreach. This is an especially significant point in consideration and contrast to the European manner of governance.

A laissez-faire approach to economics and to the needs of the private citizen, meant and means that commerce, invention, and new ideas, would and will need to be put to the test of market forces to survive and to be considered useful or credible. Christianity and other forms of religious and spiritual activities were and are no exception. Under the laissez-faire framework of society that was initially established in the United States, Christian theology in all its iterations had to, and must continue to compete in the 'marketplace of spiritual ideas' much like material goods, commercial services, new inventions, and non-spiritual ideas had to, and still must do the same.

Since religious affairs were not and still are not funded by the public purse through government taxation, nor are they funded through mandatory customary religious tithing, nor were, or are religious practices endorsed by government-sponsorship, Christian thought and Christian practices had and still must be sustained and perpetuated by their own strengths and merits in the United States. In this sense, the benefit of joining a religious or spiritual organization in the United States must meet a threshold of credibility. Within the doctrine and articles of faith of a religious organization, therefore, there must be compelling reason and something of 'viability' that would and will persuade prospective members to freely choose to become involved with the group, or for the prospect to decide to sponsor its activities.

Without state-sponsored or state-enforced spiritual and religious customary practices that must be adhered to, or even practiced by law, it was not, and is not therefore in any way mandatory for individuals to provide funding to one or another religious organization. For example, tithes provided to churches would have been and still must be a personal choice in the United States. Tithing can be done if, or when, a person feels it ought to be done, and it is decided by voluntary will to do so. If a person sought or seeks to become more formally involved with a specific religious organization, they could have, or can arrange for, tithing to be made at regular intervals, or by choosing to specify a term or predictable sum to pass along to the organization, by free choice. To build a church edifice for example, money would have to be freely given to a Christian group. As well, the physical materials, efforts, and investment of time by volunteers or interested parties would, and will need to be freely given to a Christian organization to have it constructed, otherwise, the organization would or will be required to find other ways to raise funds to meet their aims (Seymour, 1997, p. 19).

On the merit and strength of their ideas, persuading people who are skeptical of the benefit of what the group was or will be going to do, and then, if or when the organization provides or exceeds the anticipated expectations or results, a Christian group would or will live and thrive, or falter similarly by the interest it sustains or has sustained in the marketplace of spiritual ideas. This was in the case in the early nationhood of the United States, as it is the case in the United States of today. Of course, spirituality and religion in the marketplace of ideas and belief is one of working with an intangible product, so to speak. It is primarily in the sense of community and a shared feeling of well-being experienced, that is often more what leads a Christian organization to perpetuate itself in its sustainment and success. Of course, the organizational doctrine must be on sound footing and must be of an assuring nature to provide a solid foundation for a church group to keep itself going.

However, in the late 20th and into the early part of the 21st century funding for charitable affairs, including within Christian organizations, has arguably begun to take on a different kind of character. This could be because organic citizen-based self-organized groups have given way to agenda-driven sponsors. Such groups might be fronted by charismatic 'mega-church' leadership personalities, and sponsored by deep pockets and political clout, for example.

Despite governmental indifference to, and legal protection from government involvement in religious affairs, as Russell Kirk mentions in The Roots of American Order (1992), most of the Founding Fathers of the United States (with minimal difference in viewpoint from Thomas Jefferson or Benjamin Franklin), maintained that the Christian framework ought to be the basis of morality in American society, lest, as Kirk recalls John Adams' point of view:

"It would be far better to turn back to the gods of the Greeks, than to endure a government of atheists." (Kirk, 1992).

It will be pointed out that because the legal system in the United States was developed upon a largely Christian foundation, as a matter of course then, this type of legal foundation would have given Christianity a head-start in the marketplace of spiritual ideas.

What is more important to note though, is the great importance and reverence that ought to be placed upon, and held for the ability to have and to hold onto the freedom to debate, the freedom to ask uncomfortable questions, the freedom to oppose, and the freedom to disagree with other people on matters of conscience, as a foundational premise of American society. To have the freedom to disseminate religious and spiritual ideas (and political and scientific ideas) without fear of reprisal has supplanted and continues to override concepts of mandatory participation in customary religious practices, where they might be proposed to become resurgent. As a general societal norm, in places where the freedom to practice one's personal belief system remains supported, the benefit of this kind of individual latitude can be quite easily observed. Built into the character of the United States from the outset has been a mindset of rugged individualism, and one of unforgiving self-assuredness. This has created a culture where the promise is one of limitless opportunity, and very often, it is the case that American culture can deliver something of that, or in the case that it can't, newly imagined and implemented ways, at least, to try to do so might be undertaken.

The very idea of speaking up and speaking one's mind freely, has been an endorsed and amplified in the United States, which is in great contrast to European experiences historically (Seymour, 1997, pp. 62-63). It was not until the 20th century that the decline of the established Judeo-Christian framework of ethics and conscience began to accelerate in the United States (Harrington, 1987, p. 11), (Seymour, 1997, pp. 269-270). Perhaps once again, influential interest groups have found this as reason to become involved; both contrary to, and in favor of Judeo-Christian values.

Despite the unravelling of moral character in the United States, curiosity about, and proliferation of various forms of Judeo-Christian thinking and experience have fared better in the United States than in Europe into the 21st century (Pew Research Center, 2011). Where Christian thought and ideas have been put to the test in the marketplace of spiritual ideas, they have not only survived, but have thrived, and even flourished greatly. The United States being the most standout example for much of its history. With government being even perhaps only minimally concerned on occasion with individual spiritual well-being, as was previously stated, many people in the United States have taken very seriously their personal responsibility to develop and form their own sense of spiritual maturity, character, and autonomy. All in addition to, of course, bearing the personal responsibility of attaining a level of material comfort to the degree that a person and their family might desire. Because people were and are on their own to attend to their personal spiritual affairs in the United States, therefore, to the American person who finds oneself concerned with spiritual matters, they sought out and continue to seek out answers pertaining to spiritual understanding and personal betterment in the marketplace of spiritual ideas.

Since its early colonial history, in the centuries to follow, and remarkably still into the early 21st century era of lowered personal ethical standards and normalized moral relativity, Christianity remains quite notably influential in the United States at the quarter century mark. However, it can be blatantly observed that Christian influence on society has waned, is showing foundational cracks, and experiencing message distortion. As well, it can be seen in the present day that the gravity of Christian morality is faltering in its societal emphasis and importance (Seymour, 1997, pp. 269-270).

For people who are motivated to politically, economically, or spiritually to usurp the Judeo- Christian framework of morality in the United States, it ought to be pointed out once again to people with this ambition that they have the benefit of living in a system where legal and individual freedoms and responsibilities have been founded upon Old and New Testament principles. Nevertheless, on matters of Christian influence in the United States throughout the nation's history, it is in the marketplace of spiritual ideas where Americans have been at the forefront of developing new ways of interacting with the divine, and new ways of thinking about and experiencing all things spiritual. This can be measured by the number of seminaries, theological, spiritual, and religious programs of study and research institutions available to attend in the United States (Clarke, 2018). While some institutions perhaps might be of a more dubious quality than other courses of study, many programs are well established and administered by institutions with a reputable history of scholarship and purpose, meet a high academic standard, and are backed with nationally and internationally recognizable accreditation (Clarke, 2018).

This pursuit of spiritual knowledge of course has been reason for discussion of many new spiritual ideas. Many of such ideas have been and continue to be robustly debated for their merits. Many of these ideas might have come and gone, while of course, many innovative ideas have been treated in the same way but remained and become influential. As well, many old-world ideas about Christianity have been upheld and respected in their traditionalism as well. In the United States in particular, it is additionally notable that since the 20th century, when technological innovations began to accelerate, various methods of transmitting Christian ideas have readily capitalized upon improvements in technological innovation. See: (Hayes, 2007) and (Vogt, 2011) for examples of recent iterations.

With the freedom for people to be able to develop their own spiritual mindset, character, and affiliations (no matter how the First Amendment became law), in the times since its founding, it can be argued quite well that the United States has become among the most, if not the most influential nation in its way of approaching and seeking to fulfill the Christian message (Seymour, 1997, p. 19). To extend this argument to say that this kind of success has been backed by material prosperity created from the American way of life additionally, is entirely plausible, and perhaps this plausible line of thinking ought to be acknowledged unapologetically.

The role and importance of the Christian message does appear to be generally declining in North America and Europe in recent decades. However, more data from Pew Research Center suggests the United States is faring much better than Europe in terms of the number of people who continue to practice Christianity regularly (Pew Research Center, 2011). This would include people who practice Christian belief in both Catholic and Protestant traditions, as well as people who practice Christianity through denominations falling under the umbrella of neither Catholicism nor Protestantism.

In another recent Pew Research Center survey measuring spiritual development at various points throughout individual lifespans, it appears as though spiritual acceptance and maturation improves and grows in Americans as they age (Pew Research Center, 2024). At the same time, even though many still identify as Christian in Western Europe in the current period, there is a stronger trend there toward secularization. Many people who have been baptized into various European traditions of Christianity in present times are choosing to "opt out" of "church taxes" or have "gradually drifted away from religion" (Pew Research Center, 2018). Various political reasons were cited and among the reasons for general Christian apathy in Europe. Notably, another reason cited for disinterest in Christianity was "nothing in particular" (Pew Research Center, 2018).

This divergence in mindsets separated by the Atlantic Ocean, does appear to help to sustain the case that where religious belief does not have a tradition of being embedded into a nation's functions and operations, and, if particular religious practices are neither endorsed, nor have a history of being 'mandated' by customary culture, nor where people are necessarily 'born into' a religious tradition, nor even bound to religious practice by family ties and obligations, then perhaps people are more likely drawn to, and are perhaps likely to become innately curious about fulfilling their spiritual needs. Perhaps, this will result in people coming to terms with the spiritual self more deeply, and by their own will to do so.

Even though acceptance in Europe of Protestantism (and the idea of a personal relationship with God held within it), since the Reformation unfolded, has perhaps helped to relax government involvement in the spiritual life of individual Europeans, in the current period, the general attitude of American skepticism toward the very idea of governmental intrusion into the lives of its citizenry is observably a much stronger part of American national character. This is in comparison to the attitude toward government that often continues to be found European nations (Seymour, 1997, p. 19).

Perhaps then, another reason for the broader degree of continued success of Christianity in the United States bears some relation to the continued encouragement of emphasis on independence from government as a desirable character trait and way of life. While Parliamentary Statism has long since displaced Absolutism in Europe, there are still remnants of sentimentality, as well as enthusiasm for monarchy in various European nations. This includes the continued practice of embedding symbolic monarchism and pageantry into the fabric of national affairs. Perhaps due to this contrast in mindset, and way of viewing authority, the understanding and experience of personal spiritual development, arising despite encouragement or discouragement from government, has a much stronger root embedded into the fabric American cultural character and psyche.

If Christianity has been demonstrated capable of holding its own, and even excelling, where the marketplace of competing spiritual ideas enables religious and spiritual belief and practice to stand on their merit, then perhaps there is a well-earned and enduring quality to the Christian way of life. That Christian thought and ideas can withstand open scrutiny, and that Christians will encourage and welcome criticism, and respond intelligently to it, Christian thought stands out as notable in the freely exchanged spiritual marketplace of ideas. It might even be concluded that on these grounds, exploring Christian systems of belief and practice is an excellent place for a spiritually questioning person to consciously begin their quest for spiritual nourishment and fulfillment.

Chapter 2

New Testament Contentions with Religious Legalism

Acceptance of God's Law by Freedom of Conscience

The benefit of accepting Christian ideals by freedom of conscience has been established by historical argument in the previous chapter. In this chapter, the teachings of Jesus, and more specifically, the Pauline Epistle to the Romans will be drawn on from the New Testament to establish biblical argument for the benefit of freely accepting by conscience the Christian ideal of the love of God.

By demonstrating that in the absence of freely accepting God's love and God's law by faith, the alternative way to relate to God, it will be argued, will be to inevitably become bound by customary laws and concern, and to become entwined into endless ritualized practices and habits, most often out of superstition, and to feel as though in perpetuity it is necessary to remain in something of 'good standing' with God. It will be seen that performative religiosity stems from coercion through fear of social, political, and/or even divine reprisal.

That the atheist might believe they are exempt from the above will be addressed in Chapter 3 and Chapter 5, where political substitutions for religious doctrine poorly fill the need for nourishment from beyond the limits of logic and reasoning.

The argument and insights provided from the Epistle to the Romans will offer scriptural clarity pertaining to the overall premise of this book and its argument of epistemological limits of the logical human mind. Also in this chapter, the Book of Acts from the New Testament will be used as a contributing source of historical documentation of the life of Paul.

The Epistle to the Romans is a type of letter of Christian testimony. It contextualizes the teachings of Jesus as characterized in the gospels and offers both Jewish and Gentile Christian groups alike in Rome a logical and persuasive presentation of how to best relate to God. The Epistle to the Romans continues to serve Christians the world over as a pathway of solid footing for how to best relate to God. The Epistle is attributed to Paul the Apostle (ca. 4 B.C.E.–ca. 65 C.E.).

Before his conversion to Christianity, Paul was a Jewish man, brought up in the Pharisaic tradition of religious teaching. He was also known as Saul of Tarsus. The Book of Romans and other Pauline Epistles were regarded by Protestant Reformers Martin Luther and John Calvin to reflect a high standard of expression of Christian life as it ought to be fulfilled. Both Luther and Calvin held this view, despite both eventually coming to hold firmly to adamant viewpoints regarding the validity of predestination theology (Walker, 1970, pp. 315, 351, 355, 397-401).

The Book of Romans (Epistle to the Romans) outlines the Christian standard of morality, how to keep the law of God, and through Jesus, how to accept the love of God by faith. Paul the Apostle is thought to be the authentic author of the Epistle to the Romans (Tabor, 2012, p. 227). The Book of Romans is among six other New Testament Epistles that are generally accepted as such (Tabor, 2012, p. 228). It is the case however, that differences of opinion remain regarding the authorship of six additional New Testament Epistles attributed to Paul, and what his role and contribution to the Books of Acts of the Apostles might have been additionally (Tabor, 2012, p. 228).

The context for writing the Epistle to the Romans was likely that of preceding a journey to Rome to evangelize and as well to reaffirm the Christian message for people who already had accepted it. As mentioned, this part of the bible has been chosen to examine and to point out the degree to which strict adherence to rituals of religious law in some Jewish traditions contrast the offer to freely accept the law of God and love of God by conscience, as God's law is found in the Christian message. Acceptance of the law and love of God (one and the same) are central to Christian teachings and the Christian message. Paul illuminates this in the Epistle to the Romans.

Exegetical context and meaning will be practiced as best as possible in the exploration of scripture that is applicable to the arguments presented. Numerous New Testament books advise Christians on how to fulfill God's law and how to accept and to share His love. Quite obviously, in terms of importance, the teachings and life of Jesus as the son of God directly are the most important in consideration of how to understand and how to fulfill the Christian message.

The Gospels in the New Testament chronicle the ministry of Jesus, and how he interacted with people by sharing the love of God. Of secondary consideration, the Acts and Letters (Epistles) of the Apostles in the New Testament support Jesus' message for humanity and help to ensure that Jesus' teachings remain planted and endure.

It is disputed as to whether Paul the Apostle had any direct contact with Jesus. He was educated in the Pharisaic tradition of Judaism, and he was known to have practiced customary Jewish religious law with great zeal. In the New Testament, Paul has been documented as, and has confessed to having persecuted Christians mercilessly for their beliefs prior to his conversion (Acts 9:1-2 NLT) (Pferdehirt, Trimiew, Troyer-Shank, & VanderHook, 1997, p. 421). It is thought that Paul renounced his disdain for Christians after a personal spiritual vision of Jesus while travelling (to Damascus) and quickly converted to Christianity after this occurred (Acts 9:4-19 NLT) (Pferdehirt, Trimiew, Troyer-Shank, & VanderHook, 1997, p. 422). For Paul, his vision was so profound, and thus completely life-changing, that he chose to alter the trajectory of his life (Acts 26:12-23 NLT). From the point of his vision of Jesus onward, Paul sought to travel the Mediterranean world to testify to the importance of accepting the Christian message of God's love. Paul spent most of his time after his conversion committed to evangelizing those who were not yet accepting of Christianity, and to maintaining Christian belief where it had already begun to take root (Acts 9:20-22 NLT), (Pferdehirt, Trimiew, Troyer-Shank, & VanderHook, 1997, p. 423). Additionally, it has been understood and can be seen in his writing that Paul approached his newfound life's purpose with unrelenting enthusiasm and tremendous fervor.

Using the terminology introduced in Chapter One, Paul would have carried out his newfound purpose very much in the context of a hostile, harsh, and unforgiving 1st century marketplace of spiritual ideas (Acts 9:20-22 NLT), (Pferdehirt, Trimiew, Troyer-Shank, & Vander Hook, 1997, p. 423). Because it was the case that the reception in the 1st century marketplace of spiritual ideas was so unforgiving, Paul was often met with skepticism and ridicule regarding his conversion. He was frequently imprisoned, subjected to violence, and often conspired against for unapologetically expressing his views and belief (Acts 9:22-30 NLT), (Pferdehirt, Trimiew, Troyer-Shank, & Vander Hook, 1997, pp. 422-425).

Despite this kind of cruelty, Paul continued to readily and unreservedly take his newfound faith and share it directly with those who were actively hostile and aggressive toward the establishment of the Christian Church (Acts 9:31 NLT), (Pferdehirt, Trimiew, Troyer-Shank, & Vander Hook, 1997, pp. 422-425). Paul's letter to the Romans is a key example of his efforts, and it reflects his deep commitment and convictions of conscience to his faith. In the letter, Paul goes to great lengths to teach his audience the difference between keeping the law and fulfilling the spirit of God's law. Paul's letter to the Romans calls into question the benefits and necessity of adhering strictly to pre-Christian religious law and customary religious habits and practices for their own sake. Through Paul's testimony in the Book of Romans, he professes the benefits of faith and has skillfully constructed a logically persuasive document that was intended to appeal to, in large part, what was likely the mindset of what might have been a disinterested Roman audience, in addition to people already practicing Christian belief. Through his letter, Paul presents the offer of a new channel to find greater understanding of the nature of God and how to relate to Him as Jesus had taught. Paul presents a compelling line of reasoning in the Epistle to the Romans regarding problems that arise when rigid adherence to religious law and the practice of ritualized customary behavior, are premised upon the fear of God's punishment. These types of practices arise in the absence of, and contrary to, faith in God's love. As had Jesus taught, living according to law founded on fear of God was an ill-found 'old way' of understanding God. It was the way to a life of misery that Jesus sought to dismantle, to overturn, and from which to free humanity (Matthew 9:14-17 NLT).

In the letter, Paul makes the distinction between what it means to live by the law of God instead of by faith in God's clear. The central argument of the letter can be seen below. In the verses of the Epistle to the Romans referenced, Paul warns against excessive preoccupation with seeking righteousness (being in good standing with God) by doing deeds or acting to keep God's law for the sake of believing such things will influence favor with God. Paul advises and asserts that even people who do not have, or have not had, any written access to God's law may be seen as righteous in

God's eyes (again, aligned in a way of good nature and integrity that is acceptable to God) if they:

"...know his law when they instinctively obey it, even without having heard it. They demonstrate that God's law is written in their hearts, for their own conscience and thoughts either accuse them or tell them they are doing right."

(Romans 2:13-15, NLT)

The idea that the law of God is something that is felt and understood intuitively foremost, and that it is not something to be necessarily understood as intellectual knowledge from the outset, is, on the balance, a wide discrepancy in the characterization of God's law as written in the Bible between Old Testament scripture (already existing during Paul's time and of Judaic origin, but also part of scripture common to both Judaic and Christian faiths). New Testament scripture (as post-resurrection writing, is solely held as part of Christian belief).

Paul argues that when God's Law is carried out by way of the heart, God will see the goodness and integrity of the person who carries His law that way. This is the case Paul contends in the scripture passage above, whether people who hold the law in their heart have already heard the message of Jesus, or not (Koning, 2004, p. 22). It is people who live this way (by conscience) Paul argues, who in God's eyes live according to His desire for creation (Koning, pp. 22-23).

A person who lived more than two thousand years ago, who heard this kind of messaging for the first time, would have very likely received the concept as a bold, controversial, or even provocative line of thinking. Leading with God's law first by way of the heart, rather than by tradition, would have certainly been a concept in great contrast to customary habits, religious experiences, and practices at the time. Religious scholars, from various backgrounds within the 1st century Roman spiritual and religious diaspora, who would have read this kind of message, who would have listened to it being read, or who would have heard Paul profess this teaching upon his arrival in Rome, would have considered his ideas to be condemnable, as had occurred with the spreading of the Gospels with the Apostles in many parts of the Mediterranean (Acts 4:1-31 NLT), (Acts 5:17-42 NLT).

In the Roman Empire, circa two thousand years ago, there was already a pre-existing tradition of rigorous intellectual and philosophical scholarship based on the practice of optimizing the use of reason and logic as best as possible. Much religious belief and practice in the Roman Empire would have been concerned with the nature of God, and as well, gods, the nature of the 'good life', justice, morality, ethics, the specter of mortality, and of course, speculation about the afterlife. The Judaic tradition of religious scholarship originated from regions far from the Roman Empire's political and cultural epicenter but very much had the same intellectualized way to teach about and to relate to the supernatural. Taking the intellectualized way of relating to God into consideration, it is likely that the craftsmanship, writing style, and structure of argumentation in the Epistle to the Roman was composed to be heard by ears attuned to such styles of persuasive reasoning. Given that Paul (as well as the other Apostles), were jailed frequently and often met with violence upon presenting their beliefs and ideas, speaks to the controversial nature that Christian ideas would have been understood to be at the time. That abiding by God's law and living ethically would be a matter of heart first and intellect second, would have been viewed by many people as audacious and subversive claims a at minimum, and would have been punishable by death as the talk of heretics at the extreme end of consideration.

Rabbis, Religious Scholars, and Roman Priests responsible for upholding customary religious stricture at the time of hearing the Christian message, would have perceived such messaging as a threat to their claim to religious authority and autonomy. In the religious diaspora of the Roman Empire two thousand years ago, performance of ritualized acts and obedience to various religious customs and law, such as offerings to various gods, was often intended to 'keep peace' with God, or to earn 'divine favor' from a deity or various deities, or to keep peace politically (Chadwick, 1975 pp. 26-28). At times, such activities were carried out to find approval or favor with Roman leadership itself (Bingham, 2002, pp. 31-35). Roman leadership often came to consider themselves born from divine origins or convinced their citizens that this was the case, or demanded from their citizenry (under threat of reprisal), that they ought to be treated with divinity (Burton, 1912). The idea of practicing religious customary habits and rituals as a kind of offering to unseen, or 'divine' forces was practiced with the intention to keep the unknown at bay (including very much the temperament of Roman authorities) (Burton, 1912).

For many ritualized behaviors, they would have been carried out from a place of fear of divine retribution or just as sadly from even a place of fear of political retribution, as was mentioned. The comingling and conflation of religion and politics was already very much a contentious force at play in the form of religious and political practice and education prior to Jesus' resurrection, and then in the time of the Apostles, and then, continued in the time of the Patristic Fathers, these problems persisted for Christians. Of relevance on this last point, Judaism is thought to be among the earliest of monotheistic traditions. However, among various attributes ascribed to God in Jewish teachings such as the Tanakh or the Torah, God is not characterized as being an all-loving entity (Jacobs, 1984, pp. 10-18), (Hertzberg, 1961, pp. 62, 66, 182) even though these writings do contend that God is all-knowing and all-powerful (Jacobs, 1984, pp. 10-18), (Hertzberg, 1962, pp. 62, 66, 182). For Christians, it eventually became a matter of conscience and then martyrdom to decline to participate in Roman religious mosaic and polytheistic life and to profess that God in the Christian sense the only God (Bingham, 2002, pp. 27-31). Christians practiced monotheism as did the Jewish, but Christian monotheism differs because of its emphasis on devotion to an all-loving God (1 John 4:7-20 NLT).

In moments when addressing and appealing to Jewish citizens of Rome in particular in his Epistle to Romans, Paul constructs his argument for conversion to Christianity by putting emphasis on a recharacterization of what it means to follow the Law of God. Paul's argument on this point centers on the idea that:

"...there would be no need for faith in God, if it were simply the case that only those who act under direct or literal obedience to God's law were to alone receive his mercy."

(Romans 3:19, 4:13-15, NLT)

While the Old Testament is formed by a collection of works originating from Jewish religious beliefs, practices, customs, and pre-Messianic scholarship, Old Testament scripture is included into the Holy Bible as official Christian testimony as well. In its content, the Old Testament generally tells the story of how spiritual life was lived before Jesus' time, and it is important for Christians because it contains prophecy that a Messiah will come to overturn humanity's ill-found ways. In the spiritual sense, the Old Testament generally speaks of a tumultuous relationship people had with God as His created people.

The description above implies that the Old Testament and its teachings (shared by both Jewish people and Christians alike), tilt toward characterizing God's love as one that must be earned by His creation, one that is conditional upon having to make various sacrificial offerings, of being told to carry out various acts of unquestioning obedience or submission, or of having to endure numerous arduous tests of faith to their most extreme, and in seemingly insufferable fulfillment (Hertzberg, 1962, pp. 62, 66).

It is interesting to note that in contrast, the characterization of God and His Love for His creation in New Testament teaching (New Testament teaching is Christian scripture only), is anchored by belief that the life, ministry, death, and resurrection of Jesus (God's son) from death was given freely to humanity as an offer from God to express the extent of His love for His creation at its extreme.

While the Old Testament is indeed a document of spiritual affairs, focused very much on human ~ divine interactions, the Old Testament can be viewed as, among other ways of understanding it, a body of historical scholarship that documents how God was viewed from humanity's perspective before Jesus' time. That the Old Testament is included into the Holy Bible as Christian testimony, in functionality, for Christians, it can perhaps be thought of from as a record of the world in which Jesus came to deliver his message of God's love to humanity. If this Christian message is promising in this context, it is because people glaringly misunderstand, or do not fully understand how to relate to God. The difference in theological perspectives that can be drawn from the two main parts of the Bible suggest that the New Testament characterization of God presupposes that God loves humanity without limitation (John 3:16-21). This is contrasted greatly in Old Testament assumption that God's Love is a Love that must be earned, or it will not be sustained (Hertzberg, 1962, pp. 71, 182-183, 213).

This overarching contradiction in the Holy Bible could perhaps be attributed to human misunderstanding, or lack of reference point in documenting human ~ God relations (as monotheism) prior to Jesus' time. Notably, Judaism is the first religious tradition to have practiced, written, and upheld monotheistic teachings in what Jewish Scholars refer to as the "Doctrine of Chosenness" (Hertzberg, 1962, pp. 11-12)

Therefore, Jesus' life, and his time spent on earth, and in his teachings as documented in the New Testament, are the very premise for, and invitation to accept God's law (the love of God) by faith alone. The story of Jesus is of course, the very essence and reality of what it means to be a Christian; as participating in being the living Word of God. If it is true as Paul argued in the Epistle to the Romans that there would be no need for faith, if only those people who live by adherence and obedience to customary religious law will experience favor from God, then humanity's choice to freely accept Jesus' offer of God's love through him and by faith would be of little consequence:

"...Clearly, God's promise to give the whole earth to Abraham and his descendants was based not on his obedience to God's law, but on a right relationship with God that comes by faith. If God's promise is only for those who obey the law, then faith is not necessary and the promise is pointless. For the law always brings punishment on those who try to obey it. (The only way to avoid breaking the law is to have no law to break!)"

(Romans 4:13-15, NLT)

Paul is not suggesting that under God there is 'no law' in literal terms, as the last verse of the above passage might initially suggest. But rather, Paul's is more likely pointing out that the approach to practicing God's law is not meant to be one solely undertaken as an intellectual or legal endeavor, nor, at the core of this passage, is Paul saying that God's law of love compelled to be accepted. He is distinguishing divine law as something very different from man-made law, and likely, to appeal to the yet undecided Jewish in Rome on this point, is Paul questioning, even provoking reflection on the benefits of the Pharisaic tradition of religious scholarship. In this passage Paul has perhaps even perhaps undermined Pharisaic teaching directly by proposing that people have latitude under Christianity to freely choose acceptance of God's promise and assurance *"like Abraham did, as the founder of our Jewish nation"* (Romans 4:1, NLT). Yet, whether a person begins by obeying God's law *"like Moses"*, or whether one accepts it, and lives it in faith *"like Abraham"*, as a way to receive God's love (Romans 4:16, NLT), as Paul presented to the Jews and Gentiles alike in Rome, people who live *"according to law: like Moses did, are still freely offered to accept God's love nonetheless"* (Romans 4:16, NLT). This is in addition to people who have already accepted God's love *"by faith"* (Romans 4:16, NLT). Paul assures the readers of his Epistle that God's love is always available, and is a *"free gift"* to all who choose to accept it. It is, and will always be freely available for anyone who would like to receive it (Romans 10: 1-21, NLT), (Romans 11: 1-36, NLT). It is, in the act of accepting the way to God out of one's own conscience and free will and to do so, and by faith, that Paul states, that through Jesus' death and resurrection we:

"...have been made right in God's sight by faith ... we can confidently and joyfully look forward to sharing God's glory ... So now we can rejoice in our wonderful new relationship with God our Lord Jesus Christ has made us friends of God."

(Romans 5: 1-11, NLT)

The Epistle to the Romans is one of Paul the Apostle's numerous and characteristically well-constructed and fully coherent works of persuasive reasoning. In them, Paul thoughtfully considers and understands the mindset of his prospective readers. In Romans, in Paul's argument for accepting Jesus' teachings he urges readers to very seriously question the value of simply adhering to God's law for its own sake. Further, the highest achievement of Paul is that he manages to establish Christianity as a thinking person's way to faith in the goodness of God as an unseen supernatural force. At the same time, Paul manages to maintain his line of reasoning quite persuasively that leading with the heart in person-to-person interactions, is also in keeping with God's law as Jesus taught. In this sense, to relate to God and humanity by heart first is to reflect God's image and likeness to Him as best as humanly possible.

Once again drawing from Romans 4:13-15, Paul sustains his logic this way: if a person simply chose to be obedient to God, and chose to be obedient to His law solely from the conclusion that God might bring punishment for not obeying, then the choice to act from obedience has come from a place of fear of God. The reason to have faith in God, and to accept God's love (as God's law), is logically intensified at this point in Paul's argument. To obey God's law for the sake of the law itself, and in doing so, to act under the belief that one's personal agency might somehow will God's favor, then Paul's brilliance has been in his ability to clearly, and to logically articulate that God is all-loving, is not what religious legalists practice. Rather: faith (which must be directed or placed into or upon something when considering that no person can have infinite or all-knowledge) in God as considered to be a belief held by practitioners of religious legalism, has been discredited. Instead, the keeper of law for its own sake instead puts faith into his estimation of his own efforts and his own agency.

The practitioner of rigid adherence to the law of God it might be proposed, blocks the ability of such religious legalist practitioners to seek fulfillment in their interactions with others, and in their relationship with God, because over-ritualization and strict custom present an obstacle to natural relations with the divine. The religious legalist acts under duress for fear of punishment, fear of retribution, or even for the prospect of attaining political advantage, all of which do not resemble faith in God.

Where religious legalism pre-exists or becomes entrenched into the customary practices and habits of a society as performative and as symbolic or axiomatic practices, the patterns of ritualized behaviors that are carried out act as a system of societal cohesion that uphold dogmatic rules and man-made order. In these practices, there isn't really trust in God at all. In such practices, faith or belief in God and His goodness and compassion is not actually found. From such a hopeless and isolating view of the human place in the universe, there can certainly be no purpose for having free will, nor can there be much opportunity, or really, much reason to learn to lead oneself away from wrongdoing from within.

Preoccupation with earning God's favor by ritual and custom acts as an obstruction to the development of conscience within oneself, especially when religious legalism is an enforced practice, it leaves little room for people to look inward to choose to develop and maintain the inscription of God's love on their own heart from within. Perpetually chasing works and deeds to 'earn' God's love leaves little time for internal reflection. As a matter of course then, religious legalism as a practice perhaps becomes reduced to a preoccupation with feelings within a person that they are somehow spiritually 'impure' or perhaps even 'morally deficient'. Perhaps people acquire these preoccupations through conditioning from within their religious customary culture. If this is so, then until the religious legalist feels they have become something resembling externally validated, the anxiety found in this kind of system of person ~ God relations is a tremendous spiritual burden. It includes perpetual preoccupation with how a person believes they are seen by God, but, when the spiritual void remains unfilled despite the legalist having completed the 'necessary' ritual acts and offerings, such religious practices result in spiritual stress on people who believe they must fulfill religious ritual to remain in 'good standing' (or 'righteous' in archaic terms) with God.

Typically expressed through ritualized customs, actions, restrictions or offerings, religious legalism can be thought of as premised upon a dismal outlook. As a way for a person to manage their own spiritual affairs, it could very well become a quite burdensome ordeal. The person living in such a society where religious customs dominate societal affairs, will have to obey the law of God because they are compelled to do so at the heavy hand of what is unknown and feared (whether it is a belief in supernatural reprisal or whether it is a belief in tangible repercussions resulting from disobedience of societal norms).

It is in the human desire to gain agency in a world that is thought to be (and often is) composed of unforeseeable outcomes that such burdensome acts and rituals can be too restrictive to offer any sort of personal agency in the desire for personal spiritual growth. Ritualized acts might help to relieve feelings of anxiety derived from hardship and strife in the short term, however the outlook people who submit their will to such compulsions to 'get things just right', in effect become obstructed and even divorced from experiencing the nature of divine love as taught through Jesus.

Religious legalism has been the very problem with religious thought pre-Christianity, and in religious traditions around the world in times since. Sadly, implementation and practice of Christian life often becomes trapped tragically into being carried out in this way too. When spiritual preoccupations prevail, through religious legalism, the result is that people can miss consciously experiencing the wonders of life right in front of them. The result from neglecting to put the heart first, or, let alone, to not even consider leading with the heart first in matters concerning morality, ethical life, or, of spiritual health, is a lack of conscious spiritual awareness, absence of ability for inner reflection and contemplation, stunted spiritual growth, and a resulting spiritual formation that has instead been overridden by the force of fear. A spiritual healthy community is one with a longsighted view of development of personal agency, one of supportive assurance for spiritual development, and one where personal spiritual affirmation is deeply felt. Sadly, people have been motivated to act (even contrary to their own conscience), with the sharp sting from the cruel stick of religious and political fear the world over at any time and in any place. To resort to action from pessimism, or out of superstition or fear are strong human sentiments. Thought habits and practices like these can be found in abundance in human nature, and when channels of unconscious habit like these are left to perpetuate, they can quite easily result in tremendous individual and societal spiritual stunting. From negative spiritualism to negative religiosity, and from there, for such negative and unconscious thought habits and ritual practices to descend into the realm of political affairs too, it will be seen that such practices have led to, and will inevitably continue to lead to damaging outcomes for humanity. This can happen at both personal and societal levels.

If this case has been successfully presented, then the Christian way of approaching God, as expressed in the New Testament: to seek a personal relationship with God, to freely choose to trust in Him, to have faith that one is spiritually affirmed by God's love, is perhaps then an optimized way to maintain spiritual well-being. To be free from spiritual fear is to unburden the weary soul. At the same time, to be spiritually assured and content, is to open the mind toward further growth, health, and prosperity in all facets of life. Leading with the love of God inscribed onto one's own heart, made by free election of individual conscience in interactions with other people, will work to improve state of society. As well, leading with the love of God in the way described above, favors betterment of the human condition in its entirety.

In this revolutionary concept that Jesus brought to humanity, and that Paul and the rest of the Apostles fervently testified to, the idea that God loves every person individually, presupposes the highest standard of spiritual assuredness and comfort that can possibly be given. As an individual, to presuppose that one is loved simply by being part of the created world, has the potential to unleash the best standard of ethics and morality, and the potential to inspire the greatest acts of free will by which people can continue toward betterment, and under which humanity can employ individual free will for the benefit of all to thrive.

Spiritual life becomes a benefit and not a burden when practiced in the way that Paul encourages people to think about God's law in the Epistle to the Romans. Even when speaking of material prosperity and innovation, the spiritual lift from a heart-first faith can be seen in societies in which people have had, and continue to have free agency to choose or not to choose to accept God's love, and when the choice is sought to be made freely in absence of cultural or political constraints. The teachings of Jesus make it clear that this standard of interaction among people is one of God's largest priorities for humanity on the journey through the physical world. To demonstrate the highest standard of ethics and to provide the template for the best possible level of human interaction, God's example for humanity is Jesus.

On the matter of the love of God and God's law (which have hopefully been demonstrated sufficiently to be thought of as one and the same), in one instance in his ministry, Jesus was presented with a question regarding God's law by several Pharisees. Their intention was to test, even to trip Jesus up by challenging his understanding of religious law as they saw it. The Pharisaic tradition of religious teaching and scholarship as mentioned previously was the tradition of education that Paul the Apostle was brought up in. He had remained quite heavily involved with its teachings before his vision of Jesus, and his consequent conversion to Christian faith. The Pharisaic tradition of religious scholarship was one particularly concerned with Jesus' continued upset to customary religious practices and laws. In the encounter mentioned, Jesus was asked by one of the Pharisees the question:

"Which of God's Commandments is the greatest?"

Jesus replied to them:

"You must 'love the Lord your God with all your heart, all your soul, and all your mind'. This is the first and greatest commandment. A second is equally important: 'Love your neighbor as yourself'. The entire law and all the demands of the prophets are based on these two commandments."

(Matthew 22:34-40, NLT)

Being in 'good standing' with God (in archaic religious terms perhaps once again, perhaps 'righteous', or 'virtuous', in the eyes of God), by acting with integrity toward others does not mean it is desirable to simply live from law to law, as though each law is a prescribed act or axiom. Instead, God's law is meant to be carried out and fulfilled in an active way, because every person who does so becomes part of living faith. God's law has been written, as Paul supports Jesus in the Book of Romans, simply to demonstrate and to remind people of the ill-found ways of humanity when God's law is not practiced or accepted (Romans 3:19). When it is freely chosen to accept God's law to become *"written on your heart, and in faith"* as in Romans 2:15, a person entrusts themselves in their physical existence and in their internal spirit to God's guiding hand through the teachings of Jesus. To be unburdened spiritually, that is, to be unburdened from having to rely on faith in one's own limited abilities for what life might bring, choosing the love of God can provide tremendous relief for the weary at heart.

The person who accepts the God of love this way, Paul reasons, understands that he or she is free from humanity's way of ugly transgression and consequent misery. For the skeptical, this can hopefully be seen at the very least, as an improvement from being preoccupied in perpetuity with the 'old ways' of superstition and fear of divine or political will, that come accompanied with fear of retribution for having broken with something of religious or political customary 'law'.

Whether a person lives by law but not in the spirit of it, as professed by Paul and articulated above, God's offer of love will always be freely available to all (Romans 11:1-36, NLT). The idea that a 'good' Christian is one who does one thing or another a certain way, or the mindset of 'don't do this/don't do that' is a highly problematic realization of the word of God. To seek to be a 'good' Christian by doing everything 'just right' does not accurately reflect the meaning of the Christian message. Unfortunately, to carry out Christian life that way (and as other faiths are more than capable of doing the same in their own traditions) translates to living according to 'axiom' (or, by religious 'rules' in this sense). Perpetually approaching morality and spirituality by religious 'rules' is the central problem addressed for humanity in this volume, and scriptural citation and reference in this chapter have hopefully sustained this argument.

To improve argumentation throughout this volume, the definition of 'axiom', and of its related descriptors including: to be 'living by axiom' or to be 'living axiomatically', and 'axiomation' are taken to pertain to singular, declarative statements, considered as a singular rule (axiom), without any qualification or clarification. By extension, a set of axioms (or any kind of set) of intellectualized or physically tangible objects or subjects (and in the religious sense series of customary rituals or acts), 'axiomatics' will come to mean religious (or political) rules (axioms) grouped into sets of rules, that are seen to form a self- contained unit of declarative 'truths'. As well, axioms can even be thought of as perceived 'divine' truths in the absence of a point of reference, or in the absence of checks or balances it will be seen.

In religious or political language, axiomation can become a process of morphing singular axioms or sets of axioms into dogma in religious and political structures, because the move from axiomation of rules to rigid dogma is something that can quite easily be found in political form, and, because politics quite easily and quite often finds a dangerous 'friend' in religion, problems with axiomation of dogma in both spheres of life will be examined in greater detail in their comingling (see chapters 3 and 5). The shift from axiomation of language into dogma for example, will be considered along a continuum as a move from spiritual or political practice toward rules-based systems of religious or political conduct, which further become compelled and unquestionable coercion, and then can result in an uncritical and unhealthy society held together by the binding fear of repercussions for of the ugly concept: disobedience'.

The obstruction of personal freedom of conscience is found in the stick of fear used to sustain these types of axiomatic societal laws. For such dogmatics to be carried out with all the problems they entail is damaging for individual free will and the human psyche. When people are subjected to, or surrender to such systems of dogma, the results can be disastrous for societies. Carrying out rigid religious or political behavior and ritual through unquestioning acceptance of what is deemed to be 'truth', the negative effect for humanity is as described, and the obstruction to personal free agency can be observed particularly when dogmas are forced under compulsion from religious 'authority'. When this harsh description of what can happen when Paul the Apostle's argument for accepting God's love to be written on the hearts of humanity (Romans 2:15) is not accepted is taken to its darkest logical extension, there it can been found to converge with Gödel's Incompleteness Theorems. Sets of numbers translated into sets of rules (religious or political law in this case) leave morality as undecidable where closed loop systems of religious or political customary law do not permit external reference to verify their authenticity.

The inevitable consequence of being bound by rigid dogma in the absence of a marketplace of competing spiritual ideas is, that under the fear of what the law of God is perceived to be, the religious legalist has become impeded from living in God's image and likeness as God intends. In closed loop religious systems, the religious adherent does not have an external check as point of reference for the customs and practices by which they are bound. On this point, it ought to be stated that it is the Bible itself that contains the word of God, and not the person holding it.

If the framework of one's spiritual belief system is restricted under a 'don't do this/don't do that' paradigm for fear of punishment, once again, in the Christian sense, the essence and intent of seeking God is not really being lived out well at all. The absence spiritual formation within an individual is the most important distinction between *"living by the letter of God's law and living in the spirit contained in God's law."* (Romans 7:6, NLT) Certainly, as Paul outlined in the first epistle written to Timothy, observing good judgment and not reflecting poorly on the Christian Faith by one's actions and demeanor is important for Christians (See: 1 Timothy in its entirety to learn more about guidelines for Christian conduct). Modesty helps to establish and to maintain credibility when modeling the standard of morality to those who seek out Christian life. Sound judgment, mindfulness, and understanding and awareness of other perspectives in interactions with both Christians and non-Christians alike, helps to sustain and to perpetuate the benefits of the Christian path to knowing God. For people to 'not practice what they preach', Christian or otherwise, of course is well established as a discreditable habit in any way of life. In addition to the conduct of the Christian, the work of the Christian is modeled by the very acts of the Apostles as documented in the Book of Acts in the New Testament.

During the establishment of the Church in its earliest day, the necessity of the first Christian believers was, through little choice, to subject Christianity to an unreceptive marketplace of spiritual ideas. This would have been at least partially because the unprecedented events of Jesus' life took place in such a fringe region of the Roman Empire, that for the early Christians to testify to having witness to such events as the resurrection, would have been met with much ridicule and disbelief by premise.

In the face of indifference and contempt, the need to fervently document, to profess, to argue for, to persuade, and to spread the Christian story of what happened in the region of what is today Israel and Palestine, would have been necessary for the story to not be forgotten or suppressed at the outset. It is notable that the Apostles were concerned so greatly for humanity to be won over from their ills by accepting the love of God into their hearts, at a time so close to witnessing Jesus' life, crucifixion, death, and resurrection that their tremendous persistence warrants a deeper look into the Christian story by the yet unconvinced. Paul and the other Apostles adamantly and deeply believed in what they were offering to the people whose ear they had. All despite what was such a hostile market for their ideas. Yet, they went ahead and delivered their message anyway.

To put oneself at risk to the same degree the Apostles did, and then, subsequently that the Patristic Martyrs did in their era, is certainly neither a necessity, nor a recommendation in any way at all for the Christian in the

21st century. To go to the same extreme to maintain and perpetuate Christian belief and way of life in today's era, would be destructive to personal agency, and would become another form of ideology or '-ism' put ahead of personal well-being. The rule of law in many but not all countries the world over in the 21st century affords protection from persecution, harm, and reprisal for expression of one's beliefs; religious or otherwise. Additionally, that the benefit of the Christian message holds its own on its merits in the marketplace of spiritual ideas as argued here, has taken firm root in many societies over the course of roughly 2,000 years up to the present time. The Christian story has proven it can withstand and thrive despite scrutiny of all kinds, with the message that God's offer of love for his creation is there for the taking by anyone who chooses to accept it still stands.

To the skeptic unpersuaded that there is value in the Christian message, it is Jesus who points the way to living with integrity. The merit of his teachings and example, can be easily observed when New Testament scripture is given sincere consideration. Both Old and New Testaments can do this more-so when access to the Bible is put into the hands of anyone who consciously seeks greater meaning and greater personal spiritual fulfillment. When the Holy Bible is treated as an 'open book' so to speak and not shrouded with an air of mystery and awe for their own sake, the benefits to society compound and accelerate toward the good.

An example of a high-quality Christian organization is one that does not discourage or limit access to the Bible and does not discourage access to spiritual or religious materials from other faith groups that are not considered to be part of Christian belief. The reason being consideration of, and greater understanding of people who practice traditions outside of Christian faith, and the underlying belief systems that motivate and influence their interactions. Once again, that the Christian message quite easily holds its own in the marketplace of spiritual ideas. If a religious organization views the spiritual marketplace of ideas as a threat to their belief system, then the organization is not one built upon a firm foundation of faith and instead of faith being placed in God, faith is placed in the organization itself. This is a valid proposition whether speaking of Christian organizations or otherwise.

If a person claims to have faith, but it is not a faith able to withstand a degree of objective scrutiny or criticism, or, if the faith will succumb to abandonment of its articles and doctrine of belief, if, or more likely when, their faith is inevitably exposed to ideas that are seen as externally 'threatening', what is demonstrated instead is an absence of faith, or at least, a toolkit by which to rationally explain their faith to other people. In a religious group such as this, if leadership and its members feel threatened by, or are ill-equipped to discuss reasonable inquiries and philosophical pressures, they have in the very premise of their religious or spiritual organization an absence of belief in it themselves.

For anyone who would be interested in taking up the Holy Bible, for personal education, or for anyone who would be interested in taking up any spiritual or scriptural material from religious groups external to their own, personally, and for the purposes of understanding, it ought to immediately raise a red flag if engaging in the marketplace of spiritual ideas is discouraged by religious leadership. If religious literature is left to reside in the hands of an opaque or non-transparent group of religious experts, spiritual intermediaries, or interpreters, the importance of personal spiritual well-being and development necessitates defense, and requires being maintained and upheld by ardent questioning of the intent behind discouragement of access to religious literature, and the lack of transparency. When the Bible is approached as a document of historical as well as personal spiritual significance, this ensures it can be attended to with robust scholarship and freedom to debate its merit. The strength of starting with an objective look at the Bible shows its own merits this way. If the Bible is at first taken up under the assumption that it is something of a guidebook for what it means to live well, it becomes demystified. With an impartial approach, it will present as less threatening. This way, it becomes easier to understand for anyone in whose hands it will be placed. The shift from practical aspects of Christian life transferred to the spiritual ones speak for itself in its pages.

The work of the Protestant Reformation, and the positive influence it has for spiritually minded people to contemplate and question the nature of God, is carried on from the spirit of the Apostolic age this way. In both the post-resurrection testimony of the Apostles trying to establish the Church itself, and through the advocacy for personal Christian faith as established in the Protestant Reformation, the impact and influence of the Christian message has been made clear. The significance of Jesus' teachings that humanity will come to know and understand God's love, and then be saved from ill-found ways of transgression, when gravity of this message is fully grasped, it has the potential to unleash the best in people who seek to fulfill it.

Paul's message of God's law being "written" and more poetically described as: 'inscribed' onto the hearts of people who seek spiritual nourishment, has been presented and argued by its own strengths and merits in this chapter. That accepting the Christian message of God's love will drastically improve the opportunity to become spiritually fulfilled and to find higher purpose for people who seek it out and accept it by freedom of conscience has now been established from a Biblical standpoint, in addition to the historical precedent set in the previous chapter.

The Western world found its capacity for spiritual maturation by Apostolic witness and testimony through to renewed understanding in the Protestant Reformation, of what it is to freely choose to be Christian and to freely choose to live the Christian life. The dissemination and proliferation of Christian ideas by people of free conscience who sought out the New World to live their faith speaks to the transformative nature of the Christian story and is itself fulfillment of spiritual renewal offered through the Christian message.

In a world filled with distorted philosophies, false teachings, ills and vice, in a world full of competing ideologies, and, in a time of seductive political '-isms' promoted by people in power urging equivalent regard for all ideology, no matter purpose, function, or degree of internal coherence; the enduring Christian message of God's love is still very much relevant to this day because of this and is able to withstand prevalent negative ideological undercurrents. In the global marketplace of ideas and perspectives, the draw to the Christian message holds its own. The quality of the Christian way of thought and life, in its unburdening of the heavy heart, and in its offer to freely accept by way of personal conviction and conscience the message of God's unfailing love, remains as applicable today as it always will.

Sadly, problems of fear and the compulsion toward carrying out spiritual life by axiomatic practice of religious law has been shown throughout history to be the core problem with most ways of seeking to fulfill personal spiritual needs. That being bound by customary adherence to religious and political dogma has many harmful and spiritually stunting drawbacks, it is in the potential for unchallenged dogma to easily and quickly result in chaos and barbarism when, inevitably, those who are in authority over such matters are challenged, is a perpetual threat looming over such systems of rule and 'order'. This problem is compounded further when religious dogma finds its all too comfortable complementary partner by comingling with similarly aligned political ideology.

Once again in the Book of Romans, the tremendous efforts of Paul the Apostle to emphasize free acceptance of God's love, is an example of the efforts of many people since, to provide assurance that the promise of God's boundless love is still and always will be freely available through Jesus. Accepting Jesus' resurrection from the dead as God's son, and in seeing it as an act of God's love *for* His creation, and as demonstration of His unfailing love *for* humanity, people the world over have become spiritually unburdened by freely choosing to live by faith in God's enduring love and grace.

Chapter 3

The Harms of Religious Dogma: Spiritual Gatekeeping and The Doctrine of Fear

Preamble

This chapter will examine the spiritual and psychological problems that can occur when the religious character of a person and society is infused with doctrine that is premised on a foundation of fear and scarcity (religious and political, and especially notable in the combination of both). This chapter will demonstrate how the doctrine of fear is used as a tool of compliance and coercion, and will explore the detrimental, devastating, and even disastrous outcomes that can result for individuals, smaller groups within a society, and even for a society in its entirety when fear dogma is invoked.

This expository and polemic chapter seeks to persuade the reader that harm and collapse of the spiritual and civic health and well-being of people and societies that are subjected to rigid forms of religious and political authoritarianism is the logical extension and outcome resulting from law and doctrine built on a foundation of mistrust and fear. It will be posited that invoking fear of the supernatural in the name of higher purpose is a degradation of the created good in the world and is a kind of incompossibility in its diminishment of God's love for creation in the Christian sense. The choice of the word 'incompossible' has been selected here over the word 'incompatible' because of the spiritual overtones in the former, and the implied abuse of human spiritual inclinations toward good will in schemes that are built on faulty spiritual foundations.

It will be argued that fear dogma in its perpetuation, is fed by the restriction of human possibility, and within fear dogma, there is the quality of anti-human inclinations toward willful destruction of individual autonomy and agency of those subjected to it, from people in positions of authority who perpetuate such systems of societal order. It will be argued further in this chapter that fear-based ideological -isms', whether based upon religious, philosophical, or political invocations, are spiritually and psychologically, individually and collectively, damaging to people and societies subjected to these forms of strict, yet chaotic hierarchy in their restriction or sought elimination of freedom of conscience. This will hopefully be found to be a valid conclusion, and it is hoped that it will be given serious consideration by the reader, given that North American society has largely managed to subvert totalitarian governance in its history, even though the exposition of this chapter has been composed in a hypothetical manner of presentation.

Hypothetical demonstrations have been deployed because the aim of this chapter is not to center out any specific faith group, religion, national, or political cause. This chapter has been written this way to acknowledge that hierarchies built on fear and coercion are a structure that is possible to emerge in any human society, can manifest in any time or place, and is found universally in human nature as a faulty foundation to seek to uphold and maintain societal cohesion and order. For this reason, doctrines of fear and fear dogma will be discussed with minimal reference to any group, and will be avoided as best as possible.

The Void of Being Spiritually Adrift Seeks Fulfillment

In the absence of faith, in diminished practice of freedom of conscience and free will, and in the scenario of limited, or forgotten spiritual development, in such a society, enter the spiritual intermediary to fill the void caused by the resulting internal anxieties, societal turmoil, and decline of moral standards. The spiritual expert or intermediary might present in any number of ways in any number of spiritual traditions. For example, he or she could be a fortune-teller, an interpreter, a priest, a sage, a knowledge-keeper, a self-proclaimed prophet, a charismatic, a medicine-man, a wellness coach, or perhaps some kind of 'guru' or political idol. There are any number of people who in world affairs will happily lay claim to 'extra' insight, to 'extra' knowledge, or they may even lay claim to 'extra' authority regarding the nature of the supernatural: enter the 'expert'. Under such claimed 'expertise', perhaps the spiritual or political 'expert' lays claim to said 'expertise' from having earned it, perhaps through great or exclusive study, as a result, perhaps they have received various accolades or honors for their work (they and their people will let you know). Or perhaps they more-so have felt their 'expertise' has been 'earned' by way of 'unprecedented' or 'unrepeatable' personal strife exclusive to them, and it was followed by some sort of 'revelation', or experience of 'redemption' from the 'unjust' or 'undue' trials and 'hardship' they experienced (again, they and their people will let you know). Or, perhaps, the political or spiritual 'expert' is charismatic enough to persuade people to come into his fold by having received something of 'official' endorsement or 'inherited' lineage, which is supposedly somehow substantiating or bolstering the claim to 'extra' spiritual or political authority. Charismatics are particularly effective at attaining power and authority over others especially when times are thought to call for something approximating 'increased safety', or when they require 'urgent' or 'necessarily reflexive', or 'swift and immediate' response to some kind of 'external threat'. Charismatic 'expertise' becomes easily influential when problems of economic scarcity or difficulty emerge in society.

Starting with spiritual problems that arise when such people begin to hold sway in society: the 'expert' begins to feel inclined, to be emboldened, or even to feel or believe that it is only they who has been 'mandated' or has been 'chosen' to decide upon and to advise the society falling under their guidance. In terms of religious organizations, it is such person or persons who will decide what the 'rules' of spiritual practice will be. For leaders with dubious intents, they set the way by which the spiritual 'game' will be 'played' so to speak. At this point, the promise of helping to fulfill spiritual longings sought by their adherents gets turned into living out a codified system (doctrine). Spiritual life becomes religion. The 'expert(s)' (in self-referentially appealing to the authority of their claimed 'expertise') begin to decide upon what the codification system of 'rules' to be adhered to will be. That is, what the 'doctrine' of the religion will be, and how it will be structured and carried out. In this kind of scenario, the doctrine must be kept by the spiritually seeking individual and group. The spiritual 'expert', citing their 'expertise', will decide for the group when 'favor' or perhaps 'approval' from divine sources has been granted. Of course, such 'approval' or 'favor' is going to be contingent upon the degree to which the rules and doctrine of the group have been declared to have been sufficiently adhered to or fulfilled.

So-called 'expert(s)' (now firmly entrenched into societal leadership), by virtue of their claim to intermediary relationship between people and the supernatural, through their 'special' influence with the deity or deities they have invoked, will continue to provide an occasional taste of spiritual fulfillment, yet, always seemingly just a little farther along, yet always, it seems that more will be in sight, but most certainly, it arrives if and when it has been declared by the organization's leadership. This is the foundation of works-based religious organizations where supernatural reward must be earned based on the works and deeds of the adherents.

The very idea of a relationship between the human and the spiritual in this hypothetical situation has already become one of distortion. This type of scenario can easily be relatable to real-world situations. The ruse of earning (false) salvation and redemption has begun. People who might find themselves in circumstances such as these, do not see that the codification of religious doctrine has built into it a mandate for the group or individual members to perpetually pursue 'good standing' ('righteousness' in archaic terms again) with God, gods, or with any kind of deity or deities that can be imagined or 'conjured'. This kind of religious scheme, and its success by fulfillment of its objectives, is perpetually contingent upon the specific conditions of codified doctrine having to be carried out in perpetuity through adherence to various ascribed practices and rituals. The exercise in futility, to pursue something of 'divine favor', is analogous to the incentive of a 'carrot' to motivate the uncritical and people apathetic to the purpose of the organization. To gain some kind of fulfillment of internal spiritual longing, small and short-term acts must be attended to, to achieve temporary appeasement, and to earn favor from the invoked deity(s).

When the scheme begins to show cracks in its armor, and disinterest begins to arise, or when adherents grow tired or impatient, at this point, perhaps perceived individual or organizational 'impurities' are taken stock of, for 'deficits' that must be reconciled through intensification of offering and ritual. The results will be tallied, accounted for, and added up for assessment. If it is politically expedient (to maintain order in the closed loop religion), the claim to something of 'divine credit', proven worth (or lack thereof), or degree of favor from the supernatural (or lack thereof), can be put upon the adherents with greater scrutiny by the leadership. However, as pressure mounts on the leadership to maintain order (higher status, riches or retention of power), that they have established (for their own benefit) the ruse begins to falter.

Of course, the intermediary or intermediaries will begin with more fervor to assert the benefits of further adherence to the scorekeeping doctrine, although not expressed as such. For the adherent, the terms of the doctrine are implored. The specter of the bogeyman continues to be perpetuated by leadership to help play off, and to invoke greater superstitious fear. In this type of empty spiritual pursuit, the miserable result is nothing more than vacuous religiosity, and sadly, it is carried out under fear of reprisal. Where superstitious fear fails, physical world reprisal might begin.

When God's law, or any type of religious practice, custom, or doctrine are turned into a formal system of specifically insisted upon manners in which a person is required to 'act' to 'behave' or to say things not of their own choosing, whether religious or politically motivated, the doctrinal requirements have crossed the threshold into 'axiomatic' law, by those who have attained religious or political authority. Again, axiom' being defined and presented as unquestionable 'self-evident truth', or declarative 'truth' in the absence of external reference in this context. When religious doctrine is insisted upon being upheld as unquestionable 'truth', the channels to pursue acts of free conscience and to seek genuine understanding are greatly obstructed. In these situations, the pathway toward genuinely seeking God's love is going to be blocked. Even worse, the practical aspects of such courses of performative religiosity and pseudo-spiritual acts reduce spirituality to the pursuit of conformist, and even mindless ritualism. Simply repeating something for an extended period does not make it premised on 'truth', or representative of truth, if, at the outset, the reasons for doing so are faulty. The threshold for cultism has long been passed at this point (religious or political).

From the mandate to maintain traditionally held order, from the compunction of personal felt deficit (or from some notion of personal deficit that has been placed into their psyche), and under the duress of rigid dogma, the wonder of experiencing God's creation as a positive experience, for the cultist sadly has become a dismal and even dulling affair for the senses. When a person's spiritual life becomes a matter of completing repetitions of endless habits, customs, and rituals, when it becomes: *'I must do or x, because if not...',* then a person will have quite likely internalized the message of personal character deficit and then it is possible that they might descend into restrictive personal behavior and conduct that has resulted from the abuse to their psyche. Repetition in this sense is the route to stagnation and decline. Adherents may begin to believe and act as though self-deprivation is something of a virtue due to the downward trajectory that follows.

To act contrary to, or to seek to break with the customary religious law of one's community (even when not completely cultish in character) may result in the adherent conforming to customs only because of fear of punishment or reprisal from people who are thought of as having higher standing within the group hierarchy. This may even be preceded by any awareness that cultural reprisal is something very different and distinct from the cultural belief system surrounding the alleged divine reprisal. Often it is the case that when people break with cultural tradition, or breach the parameters of a closed system of belief, they have possibly put themself at risk of becoming ostracized or exiled from their community for experimenting with (religious or political) ideas that might be considered as having strayed too far from the cultural or family system of customs of belief and practice. As such, it needs to be asked: when an order of customary cultural hierarchy is established, who then is it among the practitioners that benefit from such systems of religious or political doctrine?

Or it may also be said, who benefits when religious indoctrination, and political indoctrination are invoked?

Religious and Political Hierarchy Derived from Authoritarianism: A Perpetual Problem

The turmoil, social upheaval, persecution, and often outright war that have resulted from upset to established religious order during the Protestant Reformation speaks to who benefits and what happens when established and entrenched religious hierarchy is challenged.

Yet, during the Reformation, from the willingness of people who would take on the risk of voicing dissent to challenge church authorities, new ways of thinking about and understanding God emerged. If the Reformists' efforts have been beneficial by being outspoken, then to speak of the love of God unabashedly, and by conscience, has been, and will continue to be a significant threat to established religious, societal, and political hierarchies built on foundations of fear. As has often been shown throughout much of history, people who claim authority over spiritual and political matters become threatened when access to material and ideas that challenge their practices and narratives become available and take hold.

For religious governance to perpetuate itself in some Christian denominations, as an example, it has been standard practice to appoint leadership based on premise of a particular historical precedent dating from the 2nd century. The leadership in such religious organizations will go as far as to appoint positions of religious authority and governance based on claimed heritability dating to the Apostles themselves (MacCulloch, 2009, pp. 132-133).

For many people, the concept of Episcopate or of Apostolic succession is regarded as highly contentious. The leadership of some Christian denominations pass on church governance by way of this system, and do so, despite such principles of appointment of leadership not being supported very well by scripture. Ignatius of Antioch (ca. 107-148) himself a bishop, was an enthusiastic advocate for the perpetuation of this type of church governance (MacCulloch, 2009, p. 133). The series of epistles attributed to him (notably not part of the New Testament), includes a doctrine of apostolic succession that reads:

"You must follow the Bishop as Jesus Christ followed the Father ... Let no one do anything apart from the bishop that has anything to do with the Church. Let that be regarded as a valid Eucharist which is held under the bishop or to whomever he entrusts it. Wherever the bishop appears, there let the congregation be; just as wherever Jesus Christ is, there is the whole Church."

(MacCulloch, 2009, p. 133).

Laying claim to spiritual leadership by heritable succession to the apostles as a provable concept is dubious at best as an endeavor in the 21st century. That Ignatius' epistle and its accompanying doctrine of successionism was not included into biblical canon, renders this practice non-essential to Christian faith. Granting such power to leadership by leadership in religious traditions in which this practice is upheld, is a practice primed toward entitlement and abuse of authority. That a bishop or person of religious authority would be required to be treated as something approximating part 'divine', is a very brazen example of the 'expert' or intermediary gatekeeper archetype built directly into the apparatus of the religious organization, and all the problems that come with it.

As the Protestant Reformation demonstrated, people in power, the 'rule makers', the 'gatekeepers' tend to lash out quite viciously when their claim to authority is genuinely and even meritoriously questioned or challenged. The idea that one must live rule to rule, ritual to ritual, axiom to axiom will inevitably become even more rigid under threats to established hierarchical doctrine, especially when threats rise and accelerate. Even worse, when religious 'authorities' align with political authoritarianism, repeatedly, spiritual practice becomes reducible to the threat of 'if you don't do x, then y will happen'. This type of threat proposition represents the very nature of religiosity and overtly crosses into cultism.

The compliance with such strict systems of dogma and tightly held leadership, by force or voluntarily, is sadly not at all a credible way of being faithful to God. This would include participation both by authorities and adherents. Not divinely inspired, the practice of such inflexible ways is in the end, simply a method of becoming conditioned to keep a mental scorecard of acts and deeds. This, often from the erroneous assertion that such activities will grant favorability from God. The 'divine compensation' laying just beyond the material world will be the 'reward' for the adherent who agrees to sacrifice themselves to the greatest degree of restriction or deprivation. Perhaps intermediary gatekeepers may declare reward on occasion to maintain authoritative status. Lacking understanding of the abundance of God's goodness, the substitution of faith in God is always fear of God, or at least, the fear of religious authority.

If someone is non-monotheistic in their religious custom, under such schemes, the mechanism of fear can easily be at the source of, and the perpetuation of, the force and maintenance of the spiritual custom. The favor of the god(s) must be earned for good fortune or to experience divine approval or love. Manifestation of superstition is not limited to non-Abrahamic approaches to spirituality and God. Jewish, Islamic, and Christian traditions have all succumbed to religiosity and superstition at various times and in various places throughout the ages. That Christians often erroneously approach religious belief this way is well documented throughout history. Sadly, as a distortion of the Christian message, these practices are often still perpetuated extensively in Church communities around the world.

Those who claim special divine knowledge, those who claim to hold the key to understanding the nature of life eternal, those who dangle 'divine compensation' over their adherent Christian, Muslim, Jewish, non-Abrahamic, non-monotheistic, or otherwise inclined do so through infusion of fear and compliance into religious belief systems. When living by such restrictive axiomatics and accompanying rituals, as they are enforced by 'expert' intermediaries who function as spiritual gatekeepers, the result is harm to the adherents' freedom of conscience and spiritual free will. To be spiritually healthy, and to avoid descent into obsessive-compulsive superstition, the awareness and active avoidance of such fear-based religious doctrines and practice of hierarchy are of significance.

When Humanist Philosophy Tries to Resolve the Doctrine of Fear: What Happens?

When humanist and political philosophy get infused with formal doctrines of belief, or if the rationalist philosopher attempts to devise a moral system that seeks to avoid deism and its problems, the consequent ideology created may not necessarily be on solid footing either. It might be, but most likely not.

A fitting quotation from the influential American Professor of Political Science Michael Harrington (1928-1989) from his book called The Politics at God's Funeral resonates here:

"God is dead– long live God!" (Harrington, 1987, p. 4)

This is a play on and extension of the famous quotation of German Philosopher Frederich Nietzsche (1844-1900):

"God is Dead" (The Gay Science, 1882).

When a civilization overturns its tradition of the supernatural; then through religious, philosophical, or political means, the civilization will unavoidably find another altar at which to worship.

In The Gay Science, Nietzsche's full quote on the death of God is not an optimistic view of the coming modernism and accompanying normalization of atheism in the 20th century, and reads as follows:

"God is dead. God remains dead. And we have killed him. How shall we comfort ourselves, the murderers of all murderers? What was holiest and mightiest of all that the world has yet owned has bled to death under our knives: who will wipe this blood off us? What water is there for us to clean ourselves? What festivals of atonement, what sacred games shall we have to invent? Is not the greatness of this deed too great for us? Must we ourselves not become gods simply to appear worthy of it?"

(Nietzsche, The Gay Science, 1882)

Vacuous idolatry and the replacement idol accompanying societal dissatisfaction, is a function of the substitution of some superstitious practices for others. Instead, what needs to be sought out is certainty in the love of God. People need to serve a higher purpose; it is built into human DNA. When civilizations get plundered and deities get toppled, the deities simply become replaced with new ones in the absence of assurance of protection from, or belief in the current idol. Even more decrepit as a result, the standard of human interaction and morality become immensely degraded where political discourse and ideologies of barbarism are endorsed through citing an alleged 'higher purpose'. Persecution and terror thrust upon those who dissent can become normalized practice in such societies.

Sadly, a person's indoctrination into a culture built on the foundation of a false 'higher purpose' can often miserably lead to ostracization of, harm toward, and attempts to dehumanize, or to even eliminate part of the community or society who present as somehow not meeting the level of 'purity' required by enforced ideology from those in charge. Scapegoating, resulting from this type of 'in the name of' belief system in any form, political, philosophical, or religious in nature, amounts to nothing more than the misery of divisive tribalism. Decimation of groups perceived with disdain or even disgust, and as somehow 'flawed', impure', even 'sub-human' will be used for scapegoating more likely due to their lack of conformity to whatever the desired 'acceptable' trait is claimed to be. At this point in the societal fervor, disdain for people who have been denounced in such a way morphs into reprisal taken against them. These false 'in the name of a higher purpose' ideologies are of course anti-human. They are stripped and devoid of spirituality, or, if a supernatural being or impetus is invoked, or is alleged to be in support of these ways, then so much the worse furthermore.

Infliction of harm and malice onto others through such justifications is the manifestation of the worst possible type of ideological false belief system and is a severe degradation of compossibility with the goodness and love in God's creation. Humanity's misuse of free will to seek to coerce and to crush the human spirit in the experience of another group, is the topic of numerous works of history, politics, philosophy, and theology. Specific examples will not be covered in detail here, except to express that this is and has been the logical extension of, and outcome for any fear-based system of belief when carried out to its most extreme form. This is the case whether it involves political, philosophical, or religious mandate, in its worst manifestation, when they are combined all together. World history is littered with chaos and sought annihilation caused by such treacherous 'in the name of' ideologies.

The problems for people who are seeking spiritual answers to material scarcity, or to life's uncertainties, often become much too deeply immersed into the above-mentioned 'expert(s)' influence upon their lives. Perhaps, at the worst end of the 'enter the expert' scheme is the stand-alone charismatic political or religious demagogue figure. When the 'expert' becomes sole-source intermediary and interpreter of the divine nature of the universe, and uses such claim for political coercive purposes as above, rendered upon people who are primed for seeking answers to life, and by extension 'solutions' to their problems (including the perceived 'threat' of other people(s); therein lies divorce from God.

The divorce from God will be especially harmful for people who are held back from seeking spiritual growth, fulfillment and nourishment through their 'in the name of' cause. The carrot of 'divine compensation' that lays 'just beyond' is backstopped by the stick of ritualized adherence to dogma. Including rationalist philosophers and political demagogues, people who misuse their innate charisma, or scholarly study of political or spiritual matters, whether a priest, mullah, bishop, imam, rabbi, guru, self-proclaimed prophet, knowledge keeper, self-help wellness coach, political charismatic, or anyone else who claims or exerts 'special' spiritual or ideological authority, will have special and unique agency over people who fall under their influence when seeking spiritual growth. This is especially the case when the gatekeeper is endorsed or backed by political law.

However well 'educated' on things worldly or eternal, people who exert such influence hold the potential to distort or deter the spiritual maturity of others, even unintentionally. People in such positions indeed ought to use their abilities of charisma with due caution. Spiritual, and additionally, political leaders may perhaps have the best intentions. Religious and political leaders may genuinely believe they are acting in the best interest of people they counsel, or for people for whom they create political law. Perhaps spiritual, philosophical, and political leaders are indeed scholarly, learned, and may be motivated to genuinely care for people. However, a problem arises when keeping score and gatekeeping by infusing guilt into, or implying, and willing internalized deficiency into the believer's character becomes normalized. The effects of such abuse of the psyche for people subjected to it, or held under the influence of extreme authoritarianism leads to personal dehumanization and group dehumanization through scapegoating. The human psyche is then primed toward negative action and destruction. For examples of such atrocities, please see: (Montreal Holocaust Museum, 2024)

Psychological and Spiritual Consequences of the Doctrine of Fear

Unfortunately, for the central nervous system, human stress mechanisms are easily activated when a person's conscientiousness is exploited and subjected to external claims of guilt or character deficiency. Under such circumstances, especially when cut off from any other point of reference, the believer may feel compelled to act or to speak in certain ways contrary to their own conscience. This, all sadly under duress from spiritual coercion, political coercion, or demanded self-sacrifice for the greater 'good'.

Although presented hypothetically here, outcomes from similar clinical situations are well documented. Yale University researcher Stanley Milgram's experiments in obedience to authority that took place in the 1960s offer much insight. It can be subtle or overt, but if spiritual or political customs have been practiced in the way of a falsely codified doctrine, the practice becomes dogma, it becomes habit, it becomes compunction, it becomes compulsion. If spiritual belief and spiritual behavior is reduced to mere perfunctory acts of superstitious appeasement and self-sacrifice under the fear of punishment, then the practice of spiritual life is simply reduced to conditioning in the manner of behavioral psychology. The problematic use of behavioral psychology as a method to induce desired outcome of actions, is that it ignores internal cognitive and spiritual well-being completely in those who are subjected to it as a 'learning' method.

With a focus on training subjects to perform desired behavioral outcomes, even if 'good' or 'moral' actions would be intended to be 'taught' in such a way, the matter of goodness and love being *'written on one's heart'* aspect of morality as taught by Paul the Apostle in the Book of Romans would be severely lacking. The nature of intermittent behavioral reinforcement when people are subjected to it, is that the afflicted simply become reduced to trying to mentally account for, or to guess if he or she has earned something of (divine or political) credit' or 'reward'. The sought after external approval for acts of 'good behavior' is not the Christian standard, nor even really a high standard of ethics or morality. Spiritual life practiced this way would neither be a pleasant experience nor even really a spiritual experience at all. It would be empty it would completely ignore the state of a person's well-being internally. There would be no room to consciously contemplate or to freely express one's own personal spirituality or relationship with God under such schemes. As Paul the Apostle taught that for those even in the absence of knowledge of God's law:

"...God's law is written in their hearts, for their own conscience and thoughts either accuse them or tell them they are doing right."

(Romans 2:15-16, NLT)

People being afraid to 'step out of line', to ask questions, and to seek truth, once again, sadly and regrettably, has been very much the way religion has been erroneously carried out through most of human history. Activating the mechanism of guilt or implying moral deficit is the oldest and perhaps most effective tool of coercion and inducement of fear in the 'expert' playbook. The 'expert' has the answers and is the gatekeeper; or so such a person professes. Mechanisms are put into place that need to be performed. Acts and deeds are enforced and must be upheld. Performative and ritualistic, acts of superstitious appeasement become a false binding force and tool of coercion for people as well who, when born into such practice of habit, or who fall prey to spiritual things this way, attempt to make themselves 'right' in some way. Lest they be seen as 'less virtuous' or 'undeserving' of invoked superstitious 'divine favor' in their customary system of religious belief.

Since the self-referential 'rules are the rules', and the professed 'dogma is dogma' according to the scheme, if for example, a person engages in prayer any number of prescribed times a day, at prescribed times, or engages in certain dietary restrictions, wears one's clothes a certain way, or makes the customary and necessary offerings or sacrifices of some sort by compelled will to do so, then perhaps when everything is found to be 'just so', perhaps the hopeful believer will then gain 'divine' favor!

Perhaps not.

Compound this obsessive-compulsive behavior and mindset with governmental-enforced backing, and people become further restricted and deprived spiritually and morally, lacking in the ability to exercise free conscience and free will. When a person is compelled to act by arbitrary law or face consequences, with no belief, or even hope that what they believe in their own conscience, or by their own conviction, is valid, then indeed, faith is not necessary as Paul described. Obedience to external authority has overtaken the capacity for development of internalized ethical and moral understanding. The result being that in practical situations where there is an absence of any kind of external authority to look to, people who have been 'trained', 'taught', or conditioned as such will be sorely lacking in sound judgment when they find themselves required to make an ethical decision in situations presenting as ethically undecidable.

If a religious adherent accepts the idea that they are in effect not to be trusted with their own internal spirituality or morality, then the adherent has lost the awareness that within their customary practices, they have not actually put their trust and faith toward God at all. Instead, they have merely entrusted their spirit and system of morality to the hands of the false idol of the 'expert'. Of course, divine law should supersede earthly law, not the other way around. However, hierarchy of laws gets lived out in an inversion to this when gatekeeper(s) have codified the doctrine of law into political law that must be observed or vice versa.

Fortunately, ideology, dogma, isms', and hierarchies built on a foundation of fear have a habit of collapsing under their own built-in stress that they put upon the people who live in such oppressive circumstances. Jesus was sent to overturn and disrupt these old ways that were as present more than two thousand years ago as remain today. For humanity to freely act consciously, by conscience, by free will, and by internal conviction was, and still is, indeed consistent with and central to the Christian message.

Checks and Balances: Preventing Ideology Emerging from Fear Dogma

The American model of separation of church and state shows strength here. That the performative and axiomatic approach to matters of eternity has sadly been the story of humanity's relationship with spirituality and matters of conscience, indeed has very much to do with why so many people sought out and still seek out the New World. When religiosity becomes law, when people become unable to question so-called 'experts' on issues of divine providence (or even political matters), when people are persecuted for their belief and concern with conformity to collective religious norms, then to turn toward seeking personal relations with the divine presents as the way to internally shield oneself from the treacherous ways in which people find themselves living.

The Protestant Reformers created a paradigm shift by pointing to a different way to exercise spiritual life by emphasizing a personal channel to Christian experience. By emboldening people with questions about the nature of God to seek answers in their own way, without obstruction, has been a great advancement for humanity. To freely discuss spiritual ideas and to actively and consciously discuss matters of conscience through free association among individuals, humanity has been able to bring great ideas together that have advanced understanding of the nature of reality and God. Whether people understand it or not, on having exposed problems associated with spiritual gatekeeping, it can be beneficial to simply 'bypass the middleman' so to speak, in matters of faith and conscience.

As a further point of support against religious hierarchy, Christian groups with demonstrated credibility and mainstream acceptance will often refer to the elders and people in administration or pastoral 'authority' in their church as 'brother' or 'sister'. There are New Testament references the support this practice (The Book of James in English NLT translation provides beautifully expressed examples of this type of reference to fellow Christians). As a stereotype, such usage of language in church settings is often perceived as comical or portrayed as such in popular media. However, when not used in a casual, colloquial, jovial, or elevated way, but rather, to respectfully indicate a degree of sameness under God, such references offer check and balance against risk of authoritarian religious hierarchy. This is supported further by 1 John 3: 2-8 because *"we are all children of God in His eyes"*.

While other faith traditions do the same, whether Christian or not, of course, there ought to be a voluntary self-identification component to being called 'brother' or 'sister' that would lend itself to this method of address to be credible. Freely choosing to self-reference avoids depersonalization, lest this type of referencing be misused to label or vet others as 'nonbelievers', or to presume higher standing over people who do not wish to use such language. In further support of all being equal under God, even if a person has no formal 'expertise' on matters of Christian spirituality, anybody can guide others and share their personal testimony. This is an encouraged practice in credible Christian denominations and organizations.

Jesus sought fishermen, tax collectors, and other 'regular' sort of people to be his disciples for this very reason. They were people with no particularly special spiritual understanding. However, the disciples as ordinary people were special indeed. This, because they were brave enough to walk in the way of Jesus, to learn, to follow, and to share his teachings. It is in this way as Jesus teaches, all can become *"fishers of men"* (Matthew 4:19, KJV) because all can offer personal experience. By being "fishers of men" 'ordinary' Christians can help make it known that in faith that *"there is no need to fear, for God's love is stronger than our fear"* (Matthew. 14:27-32, NLT).

The 'ordinary' person can make known that God's love is freely available to all, even to people who live to be performative of His law, or are not yet guided by faith. God's love can of course be shared with people who have not yet found their footing on any sort of spiritual path. Saul of Tarsus was born into the Pharisaic tradition of Judaism, and once again has been documented to have persecuted Christians before his own personal vision led to his conversion to Christian faith. Paul outlined the reason for God's law as follows, again taken from Romans:

"...It was recorded for our benefit, too, assuring us that God will also count us as righteous if we believe in him, the one who raised Jesus our Lord from the dead."

(Romans 4 :22-24, NLT)

Chapter 4

Tension Between Predestination and Free Will: Testing Scriptural Coherence

Message Inconsistency as a Barrier to Acceptance of Christian Faith

The Protestant Reformation brought acceptance of personal and free inquiry into the nature of God. This included freedom to uphold personal spiritual convictions, and additionally freedom to develop and form personal spiritual character. All of this became more acceptable without necessarily requiring an individual to seek intermediary counseling to find one's spiritual way.

Even though leading Protestant Reformation thought leaders premised their foundation of belief on authority of scripture, advocated for individual engagement with scripture and believed that spiritual formation was a matter of individual responsibility, it is both striking and peculiar to point out that in development of articles of Protestant doctrine, prominent theologians such as Martin Luther had concluded that much, if not all human activity is premised upon predestination (Walker, 1970, pp. 315,389). Reformer John Calvin was a foremost subscriber to the doctrine of Predestination (Walker, 1970, pp. 399-400).

For the Protestant movement itself, this was one of the most divisive issues, point of contention and area of divergence. Lutheran and Calvinist versions of Protestantism agreed on predestination as valid theology, yet differed in their belief of the way that it functions and exists. In Lutheran theology that was developed, the viewpoint on predestination tilted toward building the Church from the ground up ('soul-winning'). This trajectory started by spreading belief in God person-by-person. The nature of divine life, it was thought, meant individual teaching, contemplation, discussion, and finally, a person could freely choose to accept the love God, and then the kingdom of God would be fulfilled by believers who freely choose the love of God (Dunstan, 1961, pp. 79-80). In contrast, a very top-down picture of predestination had emerged under Calvinist theology. The Calvinist viewpoint involved the irrefutable word of God as being the absolute authority on matters of destination of the soul (Dunstan, 1961, pp. 79-80). In the Calvinist viewpoint on predestination, the kingdom of God will be fulfilled regardless of human involvement or attention to the Christian message (Dunstan, 1961, pp. 80-82).

Predestination itself can be defined as the idea that God has absolute foreknowledge, and has already decided what the outcome for every individual and for humanity will be. Typically, predestination in the Christian sense is taken into consideration with respect to who will be granted entry into Heaven upon physical death, that is, who will receive 'salvation' in traditional Christian terminology (Reese, 1999, pp. 602-603). Predestination is supported by scriptural assurance that God is all-powerful and all-knowing. However, in contention with the concept of predestination it could be a point of consideration that the third assurance of the Christian message (that God is all-loving), would perhaps be false. In the Lutheran and Calvinist divergence of perspective on the concept of predestination, the very question of personal free will lies at the heart of the disagreement. Lutheranism (as well as the Protestant movement of Arminism) tilts toward believing that individual free will to choose to accept Christ to gain salvation (Reese, 1999, p. 602). By distinction, the Calvinist viewpoint on individual free will is that a person earns freedom as a form of salvation for accepting Christ (Reese, 1999, p. 602).

This chapter will minimize and as best as possible avoid direct evaluation of, or advocacy for benefits and/or drawbacks of any particular established viewpoint on matters of free will and predestination. Citing reasons such as historical devastation and destruction caused by the Thirty Years' War (1618-1648) as one of religious rigidity, intolerance, and infusion of political ideology. Differing Christian perspectives, including that of the nature of free will were emerging at that time, and although, derived from scripture, disagreeing religious perspectives factored into reordering of various European nations as a function of the Thirty Years' War.

Tragically, the Thirty Years' War was yet another example of the human will toward acts of incompossibility rendered against, and inconsistent with the goodness of God's creation. Unfortunately, for people who lived through it, it was another 'in the name of' event of sheer misery and suffering in human history. Because of such differences of viewpoint within Protestantism, among Catholic, Orthodox, and within various philosophical perspectives, this chapter will not only seek to minimize and to avoid advocation of any particular view, but instead, will seek to shift discussion of free will and determinism away from overly simplistic and direct argumentation that the two concepts are in full and complete opposition with one another.

Also, this chapter will offer argument that the proportional weight and tension between the two concepts is not quite what it seems to be within the Christian message upon reflexive reaction. *When the problem of predestination versus free will in the Bible is encountered, it will be proposed that individual acts and deeds of free will play a much less significant role as a Christian pathway to spiritual fulfillment than people might be inclined to think. Yet, at the same time, it will be proposed that acts and deeds of free will are of tremendous significance as a Christian pathway to spiritual fulfillment in ways not immediately considered.*

Max Weber's claim that material well-being and prosperity rose in the United States as a function of the 'Protestant Work Ethic' comes into question under consideration of tension between predestination and free will. It arises in the extent to which the work and deed of the Christian will influence what happens when the human spirit passes into God's hands in eternity. Concern with acts of human agency will form the central purpose from which this chapter is intended to offer spiritual relief for people excessively preoccupied with the work and deed of the Christian.

Weber claimed that the 'Protestant Work Ethic' was a core character trait of American ethos in his observation of society in the United States. Yet, given the viewpoint of many Protestant groups that God has already decided who is predestined to enter Heaven, why would the work of the Christian then even really matter? If the preceding chapters have established a scriptural basis for free will, then assessing the biblical legitimacy of determinism warrants a thorough examination. In consideration of the totality of predestination as a concept, then would it matter how people will use free will? Surely the idea that peoples' lives have a predetermined outcome would be completely at odds with any notion of personal agency or free will. Confusingly, it can be inferred from the Bible that both free will and predestination exist, granting both concepts status of validity for Christian belief.

Naturally then, skepticism of Christianity on philosophical grounds justifiably arises in the rationalist mindset. As well, the agnostic or atheist might find Christian belief discreditable on these grounds, citing scriptural inconsistency within the Bible because there appears to be internal message incoherence and overt contradiction. Similar confusion when engaging with scripture might lead a Christian believer to dismiss their belief if they become convinced that the message is unreliable.

From Leibniz's theory that God created the universe using compossible substance and ideas, under the application of that viewpoint as a philosophical perspective, then perhaps the appearance of spiritual contradiction in the Bible would be understandable grounds for the skeptic to dismantle the Bible as itself incompossible with God's creation. Incompossibility, oddly enough, could be viewed as a charge against the Bible because it would be inconsistent with the created world if the word of God itself contained internally contradictory spiritual concepts. This, despite the assertion by most Christian denominations that the Bible forms the inerrant or infallible word of God. The jarring contrast between predestination and free will contained in the Bible presents as a standout example of such types of internal contradiction seemingly expressed in its pages.

Observably, people tend to pessimistically lean toward a belief in a lack of autonomy in their life. Greek and Roman literature such as the Odyssey of Homer and Virgil's Iliad emphasized the futility of human agency. In classical literature, the fate of mortals was viewed as being in the hands of a chaotic supernatural world consisting of polytheistic forces at odds with each other and humanity. Yet, in the logic of the Apostle Paul in the Epistle to the Romans then: without free will, what is the point of faith? If it is the case as well that only certain people are 'predestined' toward God's favor in the kingdom of Heaven, then why wouldn't the concept of free will imply that the 'predestined' people would have 'free license' to act and to do as they please? Similarly, if it is thought that a person is not predestined to enter the kingdom of Heaven, why would they too not have 'free license' then to use their free will to do as they please? This presents theological problems, particularly if their perception is further compounded to the negative with of a lack of hope that they would have no prospect of be granted entry to Heaven in not being among the predestined?

'Antinomianism' takes on various meaning in the theological sense. In the way characterized above, it can be seen that people who consider themselves predestined by God to be saved from Hell, and therefore, think of themselves as favored to enter the kingdom of Heaven exclusively, why would they have any reason to uphold moral law, or act according to it?

To people skeptical of Christian faith, this is an entirely valid argument. No doubt, predestination and free will appear to be contradictory and logically paradoxical concepts and carry tremendous theological 'baggage', so to speak historically. When trying to motivate agnostics or atheists to direct their intellect toward Christian understanding and wisdom, these types of perceived inconsistencies present barriers to dialogue and engagement with the Christian message. Indeed, among thinking Christians as well, contentions such as these are long-standing problems of clarification within scripture. Asking the logical mind to accept on faith what is seemingly incomprehensible and implausible is quite understandable.

In hopes that the skeptic might come to accept by freedom of conscience the love of God through Jesus, but at the same time for the Christian to profess that much, if not every part of human existence has been decided already, what would be the compelling reason to accept the offer of God's love through faith? Rightfully, this criticism has been, and will continue to be posited by people who already lean toward disregard of Christianity and its coherence.

For the rationalist mind, the seemingly absurd contrast between predestination and free will highlights the seeming futility of seeking divine understanding. Yet, if people who are skeptical, agnostic, atheist, or exclusively 'trust science' can at least agree that given cognitive capacities and conscious perceptions available to the individual by way of the extraordinary agency of the human mind, as 'free thinking individuals', what is there to lose by at least trying to engage with Christian thought?

Christian Scriptural Coherence: Examining the Bible with the Tools of Rationalism

Despite what the chapter heading suggests, it can be argued that the predestination versus free will problem derived from the Bible is not really a lag on Christian thought at all. Predestination being the idea that all that we do has been already decided and is known to God is very much implied in the Old Testament and is also emphasized in the Acts and Epistles of the Apostles in the New Testament as well as the Gospels. However, in the New Testament Gospel accounts of Jesus, it can be argued that even though predestination is addressed, Jesus himself minimizes the idea in favor of guiding people toward living by his teachings as the model for ethical and compassionate interaction with others.

Whatever the complexities, the balancing scale of free will contrasted by a predetermined and divine plan for humanity are competing biblical concepts. However, whether thought of being done through free will or by predestination, the focus on choosing to fulfill the will of God through Christian life and deed is emphasized in the Synoptic Gospels, the Gospel of John, and in the Acts and Letters of the Apostles altogether.

By predestination or by free will, or somehow a combination of both, what really ought to be of concern in the work of the Christian is to seek and fulfill the kingdom of God (Matthew 6:33 NLT, NASB), (Mark 1:15 NLT, NASB), (Luke 22:16 NLT, NASB), (John 18:36, NLT, NASB). *Perhaps as a function of a secularized modern western culture, an underlying assumption made by the 21st century rational mind is perhaps that free will is a concept that is in its totality synonymous with self-interest. The reasoned Christian ought to respond to that model of free will by explaining that the law of God is the boundary of permissibility under which people ought to exercise free will.* The Christian could cite responsible usage of free will is granted under the two most important of the commandments (Matthew 22:34-40).

In this sense, for the Christian life, people ought to act for the betterment of humanity regardless of God's foreknowledge, regardless of humanity's estimation of God's plan, and regardless of the degree to which it is believed that 'divine compensation' such as predestination, or being granted entry into Heaven upon passing is thought of as the goal or reward for fulfilling acts of good deed through free will. Under this characterization of Christian life, doing the work of God simply because it is the right thing can minimize the predestination ~ free will debate in Christian theology.

The Purpose of Entrusting Humanity to Govern the Affairs of Earth

What is the erroneously human made concept of 'divine compensation' if not a construct of putting faith misguidedly into one's own actions to demonstrate 'worth' to God? Similarly, to try to will divine favor is underlain by an inherently self-interested mindset and a lack of trust in God. Contrary to Christian messaging, however competent, capable, or intelligent humans might think themselves to be, faith residing in personal abilities alone discredits the belief that faith belongs in God, and God alone.

By working for the betterment of oneself and society, and the even for the earth, but in not feeling compelled to do so, to not have to 'earn' one's way to divine favor supports the case that there is freedom found in living by faith in God. This is in contrast to over-reliance on trying to intellectually understand God's law and a 'best guess' His will for creation, or how it ought to be carried out.

Although complete universal understanding cannot reasonably be contained within the human mind, as in, the human mind reaches limits of rational understanding, it is accepted in science and religion alike that humans have greater 'cognitive capacity' of mind compared to cognitive capacities of other species. No doubt, people are distinct from other species, whether a person observes that from a scientific or theological viewpoint. In the Book of Genesis, God entrusts humanity with the responsibility to govern the affairs of the earth and its creatures (Genesis 1:26-28). Differentiation between people and the animal kingdom is made clear from scriptural understanding. It ought to be pointed out as well here that the work of the environmental scientist correlates to scripture in this way, whether the environmental scientist accepts biblical messaging or not.

In terms of advanced human cognitive capacity people are also able to freely ponder the nature of their own existence. People can freely look at the stars and wonder. People have the capacity internally to freely reason and to freely engage in abstract thought, outside of what happens in the moment and in the physical world.

Is the Destination of the Human Soul Predetermined Whereas the Human Mind Requires Special Consideration?

In theories of mind, supported from cognitive research, it has been argued that consciousness enables the human mind to have self-awareness and capacity to self-observe while engaging with the world external to the mind. The technical term in the study of the mind for such ability of the human mind to observe itself is called "Pre-reflective self- consciousness" (Zahavi, 2006 12(2), p. 6), (Restak, 2012, pp. 106-108).

That humans are self-aware of personal existence happens independently from interaction with the external physical world, and independently of efforts to try or to try not to, begs the question of the degree to which determinism in development of the human mind requires input or stimulus from the external world.

The life of Helen Keller, who became blind and deaf at a young age (and therefore blocked to a large degree from external input from physical existence), may offer the cognitive scientist and also, the theologian insight into questions of how the mind develops. Helen Keller's biography details how she eventually learned to communicate thoughts and ideas contained within her mind, and offers a glimpse at the degree to which the human mind develops and exists independently from physical world inputs. This can be considered in the context of prevailing cognitive science theories proposing that from within natural-world activities and interactions the physical human brain as physical matter is thought to be from where the human mind emerges.

That determinism might be proposed to be limited to physical and spiritual experience and outcome and might suggest that the mind is the governing domain of free will, warrants further consideration of mind from a theological perspective in consideration of the experience of Helen Keller. This proposition is premised on grounds that activities of mind seem to carry on in the absence of external and worldly input, as suggested by her experiences. Despite minimal external world input, the existence of a rich internal world within her mind has been documented in her biography, upon having found a way to interact with the external world through the miraculous efforts of her caregiver and teacher Anne Mansfield Sullivan. Thanks to this incredible story of discovery, patience, and perseverance, through the work of her teacher, Ms. Keller was able to make others aware of what it was like to not be able to experience the sounds and sights of the external world directly.

From a theological perspective, that the story of Helen Keller would suggest the human mind is a predetermined entity but yet has capacity for free agency, what would the circumstances of Helen Keller's life reveal about such a theory? Also then, what do the circumstances of Helen Keller say about the degree to which acts and deeds in the physical world matter in relation to free will? Also, what does this say about current emergent mind theories in cognitive science that are in contrast to the suggestion that the nature of the human mind has been predetermined?

To develop a spiritual theory of mind on these grounds, but to note there exist interactions between the mind and the physical world, and that the intents of the mind when converted to action influence the physical world, is important in the context of the mind's ability to will people to carry out such physical world interactions. Of course, reciprocally, by experiencing physical world influences (including interactions with other people), the mind in its response to inputs from the world outside itself uses these inputs to determine what to do.

More interestingly, when examining the experiences of Helen Keller who, although had some external experience with the world of sight and sound prior to becoming ill at a young age, there is a deeper story to be told to mind theorists about what the implications are. By suggesting that awareness of personal self-hood and activities of the mind might occur in the absence of reference to physical-world externalities raises questions regarding what referential inputs the mind would source in the absence of access to physical world inputs.

Citing Helen Keller's story, the mind can conceivably construct meaning and ideas independent from sensory input from the external world to inform it and for the external world to be of influence on its development. Of theological significance, this would suggest that the human mind has particularly unique properties and that it may contain within it something not of the physical world directly, but rather, the mind might have perhaps something of spiritual properties, non-physical world origins, or even something approximating divine character or influence. This, considering its ability to still function and form ideas in the absence of awareness of the physical world and without drawing inputs from it.

If the human mind can function independently from, and without awareness of properties and inputs of and from the physical world, does that lend itself to the human mind originating from somewhere external to the physical world? By extension, if the mind exists externally from the physical world as a separate entity, has it therefore originated from the non-tangible world in some way?

At this point, if the preceding line of questioning is accepted as coherent, plausible, or considered to be a consistent set of ideas, then, in consideration of Gödel's Incompleteness Theorems (please see the supplemental material in the back matter), can the human mind be considered to have at least something of a self-referential quality for agnostics, atheists, or skeptics who are not in support of argumentation for divine forces?

Also, if the mind contains within its properties the possibility to support its existence as self-referential, and is therefore axiomatic, as in, being of fixed property (or external to the physical world, or perhaps having existed before it), what does that say about systems of mind, and whether the mind's independent operations function solely as complete and consistent?

Does this support the idea that the human mind, in its degree of sentience in disproportion greater to the creatures of the animal kingdom provide greater substantiation for the creative mind of God in the Book of Genesis? The capability of humanity to manage affairs of the earth suggests the human mind is a tool of unique quality to influence the earth, that it lends itself to being applied to the good despite capabilities to freely choose to do otherwise. If it can operate independent of the external physical world, if it is capable of decidability to be applied to the good, would this suggest there is no reason for the human mind and free will to be nothing if not of 'good substance' for creation?

Despite somehow being a part of creation, it does appear that in some ways the human mind is also apart from the created physical world. If the human mind is compossible with the goodness of God's creation, whether individual human life is predetermined, predestined, or not, why should humanity not try to use the mind to seek greater understanding of what is yet unknown, even of itself?

Extraordinarily, people have the unique ability among creatures to use the mind to conceive of things, and ways to do things that don't already physically exist or occur. At times, such conceptions occur spontaneously in the mind. Why would it be the case then that free capacities to think and to reason in such ways would not be a desirable human attribute, assuming the creations that human beings make from their ideas of their mind will be of benefit to humanity?

What does all of this imply for the degree to which there are predetermined inputs into the mind? Given its capacities to conceive of and to infuse new ideas and creations into the world, what does that imply about the mind as an entity on a divergent path from a predetermined or predestined outcome? Further to this point, and not to overestimate human abilities, although it is possible for people to conceive of ideas that are internally contradictory (as in incompossible constructs created by the mind), people can only make or create physical objects (in the sense of bringing them into existence), if the objects contain no internal contradiction to the physical world, and are therefore compossible with the understood laws of physics. For example, to manually draw a circle and a triangle independently of each other is quite conceivable and achievable, because the properties of each by definition do not contain contradiction when considered and constructed separately. In contrast, the human mind can conceive of ideas that are inherently contradictory, such as a 'circle that has three corners' (as an experiment, to try to physically create or represent such a contradictory concept of mind would be an exercise in futility). Despite best efforts to will such a thing into physical existence, the likelihood for it to be produced by the human hand due to natural incompossibility with the physical world, is severely limited. That is, in its attempted creation and relation to the physical world as it is currently understood, it would contain too much internal contradiction in the physical expression of its properties to be made by a person.

In being 'created in God's image and likeness' (Genesis 1:26), if a spiritual theory of mind can be accepted, perhaps the human mind contains Godlike properties to some degree on these grounds. This is plausible because as shown, the human mind is thought to contain similarities as per the Biblical understanding of creative God's powers. In the human mind's ability to conceive of ideas and things that do not presently exist or occur, the human mind can indeed conceive of what is incompossible. However, people are limited by laws of physics as currently understood to be able to construct or to will into existence anything incompossible within known physics, as was suggested by the circular triangle proposition.

If the human mind contains something of Godlike attributes in this way, perhaps the above is evidence to support the idea that human 'likeness of God' falls short in its actual creative abilities. God is limitless in his powers to create whereas the powers of human creation are bound by the logic of known physics. Inadequacies in expression of ideas, acts of immorality, ways of spiritual immaturity, and countless additional examples of extraordinary misuse of whatever minimal Godlike attributes the human mind might contain, all can be cited as reason that the human likeness of God dramatically, even laughably, falls immeasurably short of God.

It will be restated that the nature of the human mind collectively and individually, pre- meditatively or pre-reflectively, is easily capable of destructive action in ways that cognition is applied to physical and spiritual realms of being. Acts of incompossibility with the goodness of God's creation are quite easily able to be carried out from ideations of the human mind and it is perhaps the case that such acts cause degradation of the compossibility of creation.

Perhaps these questions of human agency of mind and action are better left for cognitive psychologists and scientists to explore with greater expertise and methodology in greater depth. However, to conclude this section, it will be restated that theories of emergent mind might not have as solid a foundation as cognitive scientists might contend.

The Earth as the Schoolyard of Human Agency and Free Will

Directing focus toward the purpose of people's earthly tenure in the context of predestination and free will, people can see the physical world as it is, and yet, people can also see the physical world for what it can potentially become. This kind of visioning results in the development of civilization and as well, results in improvements to humanity's well- being and success.

Yet, humanity is demonstrably capable of high degrees of barbarism, destruction, and ill intent. From a Christian perspective, despite human flaws, and despite capacity to cause chaos and destruction, God has entrusted people with the agency of free will to govern the affairs of the earth. However, if human nature is such that it is primed for, and can be infused with malice and evil, then, from a determinist perspective, why would God make such ways permissible for people? If people are made 'in God's image and likeness' as from the Book of Genesis, what would that imply about the nature of God, and by extension, how is permissibility of the human will to cause chaos and destruction reconcilable with Christian belief that God loves His creation? This, in the context of seeming lack of response from God amidst times of turmoil?

It can be seen that specific theological problems can arise from the misuse of free will, like the problem of evil and suffering found within the Christian message for example. If God is good, it would imply that by granting people agency over their own thoughts and actions, the use of such freedoms should be used for the purposes of improvement to the human condition, to understanding divine law and love, to reflect back to God the best possible light. Alignment with God's love is the best possible and most responsible usage of free will, and such alignment would greatly enhance humanity's ability to understand God, and to relate to Him. A distinction ought to be made here however with respect to the nature of God expressed in the paragraph above. That is, many Christian theologians emphasize God's permissibility of suffering in the world, but, under absolution theology do not draw the conclusion that human suffering is caused by God. There are dramatic differences in the characterization of God between Old and New Testament Theology, and reasons for them that factor into absolution theology (Absolution theology will be examined in greater detail in Volume 2). Nonetheless, if the purpose of free will is to improve the human condition spiritually and materially through God's guidance, then can it be proposed that by using conscious capacities to think and act freely, humanity is free to experiment (responsibly) within the physical world to discover how to best be true to God's image and likeness?

Analogous to the way God created the heavens and earth, humans have very likely been entrusted in God's image and likeness to conduct His will on earth by managing the affairs of earth as in:

"May your will be done on earth as it is in heaven."

(Matthew 6:10, NLT)

The reason for 'why' it is important to accept the responsibility to carry out God's will through human agency is sustained by the above scripture passage. Interestingly, to act to fulfill God's will for the above reason, interacts well with the description of how to use human free will, as in Jesus' description of the most important commandments taught to the Pharisees:

"Thou shalt love thy God with all thy heart, and with all thy soul, and with all thy mind. Thou shalt love thy neighbor as thyself"

(Matthew 22: 37-39 NLT)

Under such immense responsibility placed upon the shoulders of humanity this way, people inevitably will fall short of being in the likeness of God's image. That human agency is finite, and God is omniscient makes this appear obvious. However, perhaps the idea that humanity has some latitude and grace, as guided in and by God's love, the earth is available for use as a starting place to explore and interact in and by God's love.

Latitude of at least minimal free will to experiment with the physical world offers at least some prospect of enhancing understanding of God's nature and the nature of the universe. While being entrusted with managing and governing matters of the earth in and by God's love, while an extraordinary and even impossible responsibility to fulfill, is it simply that humanity has predetermined purpose but not outcome? In this, certainly there is some presumed anticipation through Christian work toward preparing for the afterlife. On this point, the idea of free will in Christian theology is supported by scripture, and on the balance is beginning to demonstrate its 'why' and it merits. Free will is a compossible construct with God's creation in this sense, even if God, in His unlimited foreknowledge and unlimited power is of course equipped to set and determine outcomes as necessary. An all-knowing and all-powerful God by definition has the capacity to include what the outcome will be when people pass into the world beyond. If God is all powerful, He has the agency to will outcomes for humanity, yet, with grace and under God's loving eye, He might perhaps watch silently to see how closely the will of human activity is aligned with His plan for His will to be carried out.

If humanity can accept that *"we are all God's children"* (1 John 3:1, NLT), then the responsibility of human stewardship of the physical world can be seen as akin to the child's acts of play in testing limits on the school playground. If the schoolyard is thought to be sized infinitesimally smaller in its scale and proportion to size of the city and even country in which it is located, then the human responsibility to govern the affairs of earth might be seen as analogously small in proportion to the management of universal affairs as would be God's responsibility. Furthermore, the claim that a specific group of people are 'favored' by God for Heaven over others is diminished under 1 John 3:1. As mentioned in the Book of Romans, God's love is freely available *to all* who seek it. If this forms a composite picture of humanity's place in the eyes of God, perhaps then humanity's self-sense of inflated proportionality is distorted from humanity's own erroneous perspective.

For example, if human responsibility is limited to tend to the physical world is as much as humanity is entrusted by God to manage, then just as children gain greater responsibility from their teacher at school for more responsibility as they become more knowledgeable, aware, and capable, so too might people attain greater spiritual maturity by being entrusted to manage the affairs of the earth while God guides and watches on.

Predestination in Consideration of Heaven and Hell: On Divine Justice and Acts of Free Will in Context and Proportion

If the limit is the physical world for humanity's entrusted responsibility, perhaps then, people might come to believe that using free will in the best possible way will have given sufficient demonstration of the goodness of individual and collective human acts? This might be presumed to be beneficial to offer to God to appeal to His mercy and grace. With respect to what happens to the human spirit when a person's physical end arrives, the contentious term 'divine compensation' surfaces here. Divine compensation can be perhaps thought of as the human spirit's 'reward' for the physical person's work and suffering during time on earth. Some kind of eternal reward is anticipated by people who believe in such accounting schemes. Under such schemes, the hopeful is thought to receive reward on the balance of individual good deeds and work as thought to be evaluated by God, in contrast to individual transgressions during time spent on earth. The hopeful believer in such a system would offer the sum total of their 'worth' to God as a measure of 'spiritual merit' upon physical passing.

This is as though individual good deeds are a method by which a person might influence God toward the individual receiving something of a 'deserved' 'eternal payment'. In presenting their case, the believer in the rewards of divine compensation would hope to persuade God that their acts and worth are sufficient to grant them something of an experience of the sublime nature of Heaven. Satirically, perhaps there would be an 'accounts payable' desk in Heaven to settle what the believer of the scheme maintains they are owed. Conversely, and with a more serious tone and gravity, in terms of barbarous acts of free will, perhaps 'hell' in this sense is reserved for those who are deemed by God to be the worst by deed among humanity. For people in whom there would be no redemption is for God, and for God alone to decide.

This is where a sense of proportion matters deeply if the idea of 'divine compensation' or 'just compensation' as it is also termed, is in any sense valid. For example, perhaps for the worst of humanity, the anti-human, the most wicked, for people in that circumstance, God would decide for such people to know hell. Those would be people in as situation where they might have committed such extreme harm against humanity, such malice, such evil, such destruction, and therefore have inflicted such suffering against their fellow person, that their heinous acts were done in severe degradation of compossibility within the goodness of God's creation. As well, in having done such acts with flagrant disregard for God's law, perhaps God would consider in foreknowledge a reserved spot for such people in a such a place as hell. Various 20th century despots might fit the requirement for the necessity of hell; again of course, that is for God to decide.

For the rest of humanity, under 'divine' or 'just compensation' belief, if it is such a thing at all, many errors of humanity's ways would indeed be forgivable by God's grace through Jesus, as according to Christian scripture. Who among humanity has not made transgression? Has had a lapse in judgement? Who has not in some way wronged another, either intended or not? It is in the question of magnitude, in the act of acknowledging the wrongdoing and then in making proper restitution, that the significance of proportion of deed might matter. But, in acknowledgment of one's errors, and in seeking forgiveness, perhaps it is likely that most people that walk the earth would be allowed to enter the kingdom of Heaven so to speak anyway. This being supported by the sense of the law of God being 'inscribed on their hearts' as per Romans. Important here is in the choice to freely accept the love of God. For in being part of God's creation, people are indeed compossible with God's nature, even if having misused free will. Transgression is limited at this point to the physical world. Perhaps such transgressions (but not too many) can be seen as an opportunity for spiritual growth and toward spiritual understanding and maturity. This being analogous to the earlier schoolyard example.

Below, analogous reasoning further shows that most people with good intent, who act in good faith, who acknowledge when they have wronged another, and then by seeking forgiveness, can feel assured that their spirit will experience something of the sublime in the inevitable event of passing into eternity. The comparison drawn below illustrates the point that much of what good people freely choose to do is forgivable in the event that it causes harm:

In the Western tradition of law, most legal matters fall into something resembling 'civil' law, and 'criminal' law. In civil law, under which a harm or transgression has been made, the restitution for wrongdoing is decided on the balance of probabilities. That is to say that both parties involved in a dispute might have had some degree of culpability, or even if only one of the parties solely committed harm against the other, a Judge would use the balance of probabilities to decide the wronged party's 'just compensation' proportionally to what happened. The offending party would then have to make appropriate restitution on the balance of what is determined to be sufficient.

In God's eyes, perhaps, for most, as simple people in having broken faith with Him, we are capable of redemption through righting the wrong. In reaffirming acceptance of Jesus into their hearts, surely, it can be proposed that for most generally good-natured people, what has been done is forgivable under God's compassionate mercy and grace.

In contrast, using any of the perpetrators of 20th century acts of genocide as an example, perhaps in those situations, for people who carried out such heinous anti-God, anti-human acts would be evaluated under some sort of 'criminal law' framework as mentioned above. Regarding their spirit upon physical end and perhaps in God's eyes, simply in their guilt or perhaps in what little there would be to redeem of their spirit due to having inflicted such atrocity, perhaps God would decide their eternal 'compensation' in a very different way with a very different outcome. Again, this of course, is God's decision alone.

For the rest of humanity, there is perhaps not much to be concerned about in this regard. Other than to genuinely and freely choose to act in the best possible way to live in the teachings of Jesus in interactions with each other, and of relatable concern would include aspiring to act toward the best possible human ~ divine relations.Relating back to Paul and his letter to Romans once again, God's offer to accept Him by faith is free no matter if we l ive by the literal law, or have it *'inscribed onto our hearts'*.

On the Erroneous Choice of Finite Mathematics to Measure the Infinite Love of God

Inasmuch as humans can harm each other, humanity has been entrusted with free will while on earth and only limited to physical world affairs. While humans are certainly capable of warring and murderous ways, the human spirit upon encountering or acting out such worldly harm or good belongs to God to manage when it is passed on from its time in the physical world.

In this way, the nature of faith is to trust in God and be accepted by His grace. As shown above, for individual concern with being received well upon spiritual passing is indeed a tremendous act of faith. In consideration of what a person might consider God to have predetermined for them, or considering what a person might believe about God's regard for their experiences and acts during their time spent on earth, questions still arise regarding free will in the Christian context. For example, if free will is thought to form at least part of earthly experience and is thought to be desired by God for humanity to carry out in a good way, then, in the context of predestination, what degree would it matter to live for this world if everything is thought to be predetermined? If this world is meant to be a place to prepare for what comes next when the human body fails but the spirit passes on, why would the choice to freely accept the offer of God's love on faith be relevant if God has foreknowledge of, and has already determined a person's spiritual path upon death? In this context, does the Christian's life and deeds logically then really serve any kind of contingent role upon passing from this earth? Confusingly though, wasn't antinomianism already discredited under the proposed parameters for the Christian usage of free will? Confusingly further, in divine compensation theology, the belief that divine favor can be bargained for, earned, or willed through actions and/or deed seems to be of little importance or sway as well.

At the very limit of human understanding of free will and determinism in the biblical/scriptural sense, under all of the above proposals for how a Christian would consider using free will, Jesus still teaches that God's offer of love remains freely available to all. So, why would there be any real reason to fulfill the Christian to love God and fellow person, under all things considered above?

In the Christian sense it is really not humble or appropriate to seek to guess the mind of God, yet many philosophers throughout history have wrestled with free will ~ determinism theory and debate from all walks of life. From a Christian scriptural perspective, the free will ~ determinism debate is perhaps more easily reconciled, at least minimally, than might be generally believed. In the Bible, the prospect of reward for fulfilling God's work, unsurprisingly does not come from the work of human intellect or labor. But rather, and perhaps oddly, faith in God can be revealed to be profoundly, yet sensibly justifiable in a mathematical sense to understand what is to be received upon physical passing. However, the kind of mathematics used to understand whatever the meaning of 'divine compensation' is, is perhaps not so through the usual way of thinking mathematically.

The Accountant: Estimating, Adding and Subtracting

A calculating person might suppose to intentionally wait until one's own physical end is foreseeable, to wait to accept God's offer of love, because God's love will be available at that time anyway. Questions of technicality arise in this scenario about free will usage in relation to how a person would be accepted after physical death. The problem of how free will has been used arises in terms of authentic acts of conscience. If it has been seen that human free will is not of the magnitude or importance that people might think it to be, as mentioned, except perhaps where the teachings of Jesus and the fulfillment of God's law of love have been disregarded so very reprehensibly and contrary to Jesus' teachings to be no longer compossible in substance or idea with the goodness of creation, would cause problems for the accountant of acts and deed. Within mental accounting games people play with their acts and deeds, for this, and for various other reasons, in the example above is seen a scheme of calculated self-interest, and there appears to be an overestimation of the understanding of numeration and number sense at play.

The Gambler: Rolling the Dice with Finite Probability to take a Chance with Infinite Wisdom

Misinterpretation and over-estimation of the degree to which people resemble God or think of themselves as 'god-like', might be analogous to gamblers who go to the casino to 'win big' or even to try to 'beat the house' even when they believe they might have a winning 'system' to do so. Sadly, for such people, the cards are not stacked in their favor. Sorry, but the owner of the house has already predetermined that on the balance of probability gamblers lose. human ~ divine relations matter in terms of best intent here too. No matter how intelligent someone might be or how powerful a microchip or computing system might be that they have built, humility offers clarity for people who recklessly might seek physical world powers that are beyond what they might be able to reasonably handle. When a genie is out of the bottle he might by very powerful, but he will not necessarily be wise or loving, and certainly will not be any of these things in any absolute sense. Simple and small actions of goodwill are a greater reflection of individual character, than are attainment of great powers or knowledge that exceed the human capacity to reasonably and to responsibly handle.

The casino analogy reveals limits. People have physical world understanding of finite mathematics and at best perhaps theoretical understanding of abstract mathematics similarly. To seek to use finite human mathematics and/or limited or minimal human understanding of intangible concepts, and then to believe that it is somehow possible to attain, to approximate, or to even usurp infinite understanding of infinite possibilities is a glaring oversight in the concept of proportionality in mathematics, and along with it, an underestimation more specifically what a mathematical concept like infinity really means.

Misinterpretation and over-estimation people have and engage in with respect to the degree and proportion to which humanity actually resembles God, is upheld in the analogy of over-confident gamblers who go to the casino to 'win big' or even to 'beat the house' in this sense. It is simply not possible to use limited and finite human understanding to seek to 'game' infinite understanding of the infinite wisdom, power, and love of God Himself.

The Scientist: Measurement, Data, Geometry, and Spatial Sense can Evaluate Universal Properties but not Understand Universal Purpose

Returning to the omniscience of God, to assume that as mere people who have been created 'in God's image and likeness' that it means we very closely approximate God in magnitude of human ability is hopefully beginning to show its naïveté. To assume too favorably the degree to which people bear resemblance to God is not however, possibly a measurable concept. However, in estimation, at some point in a person's life, they will begrudgingly become humbled, and realize that human capabilities are immeasurably in diminution to God's abilities. Perhaps God sees the unbridled pride taken by people in embarrassingly minuscule knowledge acquired and thought to be understood about the universe. How much is really known? Including the size of the universe, how it came into being, and the properties and principles that might govern its reality?

That is to say that humans can continue to measure, to describe, and to map the topography of the universe that can be tangibly and even indirectly and inferentially observed and considered. However, for the universe to have been created by a limitless source, or to have been perhaps formed by some great 'un-cause' implies that the universe itself is quite possibly limitless or possibly limitless as well. Thus, to observe, to measure, to compile data, to map, to graph, to create models for what is or has been created from or by a source of infinitely conceivable possibilities (including from knowledge, power, and love to create ideas and substance both compossible and incompossible), whereas humans can explain and create perhaps only consistent within understood laws of physics, is proportionally to say that people (in finite physical form) will have great difficulty comprehending the sheer totality of creative work that has been involved.

Finding Meaning and Purpose in the Context of Predestination: Jesus Leads the Way

On Existentialism, Nihilism, and Absurdism in Relation to Determinism

If the list of those who will enter the gates of Heaven has already been decided, neither faith in God, nor abiding by God's law, would matter at all. Also, if the limits of human suffering stop at physical death, then the commandments teaching people to not harm each other wouldn't really matter either. So, such is the problem with predestination then: does nothing of what people do on earth really matter, or does it?

If determinism is proportionally of vastly greater importance in a person's existence and spiritual outcome, then the lack of personal agency implied in this kind of existence would subject human motivation and will to futility, then fatalism would be the best human view to take of the divine, much like in Greek and Roman literary heritage. However, finding meaning in limited human knowledge, understanding and existence is a tremendous human preoccupation. This is true for adherents to many systems of spiritual, religious and rational belief that are contradictory to each other, and for people who in the same limits of knowledge and understanding as everyone else direct faith toward political '-isms' to seek belonging, whether soundly premised or not.

To believe that determinism alone is the dominant existential reality and system or principle governing universal reality would make the search for meaning and purpose an absurd prospect, whether determinist belief is attached to a god-figure or not.

It has been established that acts of free will perhaps do not matter or influence God in the degree to which people might believe, although they would perhaps be important to God in other ways. With exception to acts that are a degradation to the goodness of God's creation described previously as in, acts of incompossibility, as mentioned, responsible use of free will is not analogous to 'free license' (free to do whatever you want). The term 'antinomianism' has historically been a politically loaded, quasi-religious, over-used doctrinal term with negative connotations. It is a term that has been tossed around as a charge against and among various groups, politically and religiously, historically at various times. It was deployed previously on the question of absurdism in the determinist model of existence, and is relevant again here.

When the term antinomianism is stripped of its historical connotation, and is instead objectively utilized to balance hardline determinist viewpoints, it shows its strengths. In this regard, a strict determinist view or even predestinarian view of creation aligns too closely with absurdism because there would be no need for any kind of laws (divine or otherwise) to govern affairs because of the is/ought idea that the universe and its events are simply unfolding as they are supposed to be. The only universal reality would be the static doctrine of 'as it is' so to speak. Yet, there is a need for law, because people simply may not do what they please when it detrimentally affects others.

May it be presented: if a Christian model of principles of universal governance can be accepted, then the tension between competing ideas of determinism/predestination and free will is more easily reconcilable than people might come to believe. That is to say that perhaps it is in simply striving to be more like God that people have the responsibility to do simply that which is right, and to do that which is right is to act with justice, mercy, and compassion toward fellow men and women, even when situations present as morally ambiguous.

To do that which is 'right' is intentionally being deployed axiomatically here (despite intentional attempts previously to avoid hardline absolute and axiomatic language as a form of explanation and understanding throughout this book)! The intentional and overt deployment of the axiom of 'right' or 'rightness' (*but not righteousness!), or to propose there is something in universal understanding of that which is 'right' or 'the right thing to do' as principle or property of universal and moral truth, is to imply and to propose here that morality is not a relative term and to discredit the absurdist view of free will and determinism.

Therefore, for a person to do what is right with disregard for any anticipation of compensation, or with disregard in the expectation of reward for goodwill from deeds, or to do right regardless of belief in predestination, is to exert human will as a force of not only acts of good, but wills human greatness upon the universe. Such exertion of human will, selfless, and without seeking favor is proposed here to be the best possible purpose for the use of free will, and reflects back to God the best possible human likeness and image of Him.

The following vignette illustrates how, in simple terms, Jesus powerfully renders the debate over predestination and free will moot.

For some, there is a glaring lack of insight into the nature of infinite love with respect to the expectation of divine reward. The same lack of insight exists in the belief of having been chosen exclusively and distinctively over others to receive divine favor, as it does in those who believe they must work to earn it. How God answers the question of what it means to fulfill the Christian message is perhaps illustrated quite well in the following parable of Jesus:

The Parable of the Vineyard Workers

∞ Jesus Teaches that Doing What is Right because it is the Right Thing to Do is the Work of the Christian ∞

Jesus teaches his disciples that *"the Kingdom of Heaven is like the landowner who went out early one morning to hire workers for his vineyard."*

(Matthew 20 1:16)

Quoted and paraphrased:

Through the course of the day on which the story takes place, the landowner first finds men ready to work at the earliest part of the day and hires them for the usual sum. He returns a little bit later to where workers usually gather. Upon each visit the landowner takes to finding more workers. He finds and hires more workers to come to the vineyard to work. It is getting later and later in the day. Yet, there are still new workers who arrive and are standing around seeking purpose by looking for work. They too are invited to come to work in the vineyard. Over the course of the day, the earliest of the workers begin to worry if they have made a good decision to work for the landowner. They start assessing and mentally calculating, or perhaps grumbling to each other about the situation of seeming unfairness while they work. Human nature being what it is, they have concerns. They have toiled, perhaps in the hot sun all day. They have labored the longest in their day as well. As such, perhaps from their perspective and understanding, they are justifiably concerned about the proportion of money that will be given to them at the end of the day. In the earthly world, compensation is typically granted as such. That is, payment is received based upon the number of hours worked, efforts, and the quality of labor. In human affairs, pre-arranged and agreed written contracts are formed to clearly outline the terms of compensation for work. This is all understandable because in worldly mathematics and accounting, wages are drawn from finite resources. As such, when competing for scarce material resources, it is human nature to be curious about what other people have received for their toil as well. At the end of the day's duties, the workers line up to receive what they have earned. To the workers who started first, the landowner makes what seems to be an unfair and incomprehensible decision. The landowner decides to pay the workers who arrived later to work in the vineyard, and who worked for a shorter period of time first! Not only this, but the landowner also decides to pay them the same sum as the workers who started earliest! That is, the landowner pays a full and complete day's wage to the latecomers! This is the very same compensation that the earliest and most eager of the workers agreed to receive, and perhaps they thought they would be entitled to special consideration due to being chosen first by the landowner. The first workers understandably feel quite put off. They are frustrated. Perhaps even feeling discouraged and enraged. So, they complain. They question the landowner's decision, for they were indeed expecting something more. Something more in fact than to what they themselves had initially agreed. From one of the workers disputing the landowner: **"Those people"** *(the last to arrive)* **"worked only one hour, and yet you've paid them just as much as you paid us who worked all day in the scorching heat."** *(Matthew 20:12 NLT). The landowner promptly and firmly replied to the man:* **"Friend, I haven't been unfair! Didn't you agree to work all day for the usual wage? Take your money and go. I wanted to pay the last worker the same as you. Is it against the law for me to do what I want with my money? Should you be jealous because I am kind to others?"**

Sourced from: Matthew 20:15 (NLT).

What Constitutes Justice and Fairness in Fulfilling the Work of God? Contextualizing Matthew 20:15: Divine Mathematics Is Different from Human Mathematics

There are several components to unpack in the parable for people who are critical of this seemingly unfair and unjust way that God went about compensating those carrying out His work. The first being the ability to distinguish between material compensation and divine compensation. The former kind of compensation is drawn from finite resources, is scarce and uncertain. The latter kind of 'compensation' is quite different. It is drawn from an all-powerful, all-knowing, and all-loving source. That is, what is given from God's goodness and grace is boundless, infinite and unlimited. That is, there is more than enough for everyone.

Infinite mathematics is not very easily conceivable for humanity. The sheer futility and absurdity of mere men trying to calculate, or to in any way try to understand the idea of what divine compensation really means is shown here. Humanity's perception remains blinded by the material world as a reference point. This, even though people are capable of abstract reasoning and imagination, and even though, people can see things clearly in other situations that are as they are, and then can conceive of what they can become as well.

Nonetheless, the idea that divine compensation is a scarce and limited resource has likely emerged out of scarcity of material resources in the physical world, in the original separation of humanity from God, and in seeking the way back to Him. Drawing from an infinite source means of course there is more than enough of God's love for all to enjoy. The extraordinary courage it takes to put one's faith to God, without expectation, without seeking special consideration, but to simply have faith that what God does with your spirit upon passing is his Will, is to be freed from the burden of working to earn a place in Heaven. This, especially if free will is thought of as an absolute, which has not been discussed as thoroughly in this chapter. To do what is right because it is right, if entry into Heaven is thought to be a predetermined favorability of outcome is, to be freed from what is really guesswork or an assumption about the Will of God. Therefore, by the same intention to do what is right because it is the right thing to do, even when holding a determinist/predestination viewpoint is to be freed by faith in God and his wonderful grace as well.

The Work of the Christian & The Wonder of Creation

Is Christian life to be one of work alone? What about using free will to not only work, but to experience joy? Perhaps overemphasis on what the work of the Christian ought to be, has left this chapter lacking in discussion about what it means to seek out the wonder and joy in God's world and to remind that to take in conscious joy by experiencing God's creation is a benefit of being part of the world created for the good. The work of the Christian is certainly not meant to be implied to be drudgery at all. The joy of being alive is all around. The boundless joys and wonders to consciously experience in the natural world and beyond surely are limitless when a person is attuned to the miracle that is life itself.

The idea of limiting the discussion of free will to work and 'just compensation' either materially or spiritually is quite extraordinarily laughable in the richness of human possibility of experience. Pessimistically trying to 'calculate' what proportion of divine compensation to which one can lay claim amounts to an exercise in comical absurdity similarly. As though human scorekeeping or mental accounting found in some religious practices as discussed in Chapter Three can even begin to account for the limitless wonders of the natural world.

Due to lack of faith, it can be forgotten that the infinite richness of God's love is not at all a scarce or finite resource. The human brain can make the leap to logical fallacy of scarcity mindset quite easily. Human understanding can be perhaps thought of as a mirror image of God's knowledge this way. That the human viewpoint is quite pessimistic about assurance of God's love can find its way into how human affairs are often and typically undertaken in this regard.

Humanity may have come to believe in having developed a high degree of mathematical prowess. People may believe it to be possible to tally up the sum of personal worth to the divine, or worse, in the negative, perceived lack thereof in God's eyes. Yet, the sum of mathematical abilities as mere humans inevitably falls immeasurably short of completing the task of measuring the omniscience of God. Consciously experiencing in awe, with humility, and with thankfulness the wonders and beauty of the miracle that is God's universe is true compensation enough and is uncountable.

An Alternate Proposal to Free Will ~ Determinism as a Model of Christian Existentialism: Convergence ~ Divergence Theory of Body and Spiritual Experience and Outcome

For a person to be spiritually and materially fulfilled, it is necessary to acknowledge there is more than there seems to be to the tension between free will and determinism. Perhaps, to help minimize theological concerns for the determinism vs. free will paradox in scripture, it would be beneficial to turn Christian attention to a more ontological focus, and that is of spiritual and physical outcomes for humanity.

To fully comprehend the nature of how the spiritual and physical selves are related to each other and how they are integrated or become separated, to see the determinist ~ free will paradigm on a deeper plane perhaps Christian philosophy could put attention toward moments where spiritual and physical existence converge and diverge for greater insight beyond what determinism ~ free will existentialist models can provide. Examples of spiritual and physical convergence may include realizing that a child has been conceived, Additionally, at the moment of birth of the new life, spiritual and physical ~ convergence and divergence can be argued at a meeting point. Similarly, then, returning to God at the event of physical death is an example of physical ~ spiritual divergence.

All that happens before a person was born, during a person's time on earth, in their experiences and acts on earth, and, as well, what happens after a person's spirit makes its departure from its physical self at death might open new possibilities of understanding if these events are looked at with the lens of free will and determinism. Also, understanding more deeply these crossover points, the degree of integration between spiritual and physical existence in human ~ divine relations on this plain of knowledge seeking might help people to attain a greater experience of closeness with God.

To propose to supplant the predestination vs. free will debate with an exploration of the nature of spiritual/physical ~ convergence/divergence would perhaps be of more benefit in understanding the nature of human purpose and experience, and to better attend to spiritual and physical outcomes where the free will vs. determinism debate falls short. Shifting focus of interest away from predestination ~ free will as a function of personal agency in contrast to personal alignment with God's foreknowledge and will, might offer greater clarity on many of concerns of human ~ divine relations similarly.

Conclusions: Scripture can be more Accessible by De-emphasizing Tension Between Predestination and Free Will to Change how Human ~ Divine Relations are Discussed

It is simply not possible to calculate or to use mathematics alone to understand the immense and infinite proportion of the scale of God's divine nature and capabilities. Additionally, it is not even possible really in human understanding to know the immense and infinite proportion of what constitutes the nature of the 'physical' universe. That people believe in human capability to that degree in the current period of human history, perhaps might suggest more so of a 'mathematical' measure of human arrogance or pride.

There is no logical capability yet developed by humanity to carry out such a task as to determine what infinite abundance really means. Perhaps because of material advancements in the 21st century many people have come to believe that they have little use for a spiritual relationship with God. In the West, many people have become decoupled from the spiritual part of existence. A contributing factor in the decline of spiritual contemplation would likely be seemingly unlimited abundance of advanced material prosperity.

That humanity has improved in ability to fulfill material needs by yielding increasingly more from the finite world, many people perhaps erroneously believe it follows that a spiritual relationship with God is irrelevant. This messaging perhaps often trickles down from 'sages' in silos of higher education, and through popular and politicized discouragement of spiritual discussion in favor of explaining human intangible experiences through psychologizing. Material improvements are a reflection and testament to the inventive human ability to create and fulfill an elevated level of comfort and physical prosperity, yet this wonderful accomplishment does not imply that spiritual fulfillment and nourishment are no longer necessary.

In the West, and in many places in the world rightly aspiring to high levels of material prosperity, spiritual fulfillment is being neglected. It is being neglected both by people not being aware that it is possible to contemplate their own spirituality, and in taking free will to mean disregard for law of the God of love. Finding fulfillment and reliance on faith in self alone can result in spiritual burnout, and physical burnout additionally. Perhaps being materially fulfilled, people have become so detached from their internal spiritual life that many people are not even consciously aware of the idea of a spiritual self.

The vacuous way in which a lack of spiritual connection to God has a detrimental effect on personal health and well-being of individual and society is astounding to observe. Examples can be found easily where people in the West zealously jump at the opportunity to seek fulfillment of self in the '-isms' of politics and ideology. An argument could be made that in the West, many such political movements are morphing from the political sphere into the sphere of religiosity and then taking on dogmatic character in their absence of meaningful spiritual fulfillment.

Erroneously, when people do accept spirituality as part of their experience, many have drawn the connection that finite material satisfaction is somehow extended to being owed divine compensation when they go seek spiritual satisfaction. That mathematical accounting schemes could be found, such as measurement or tallying, that could be calculated to understand the role of predestination and free will, is works-based theology, and on those grounds divine compensation theology is faulty in appraisal as a kind of religious indoctrination in containing attributes of cult-like religiosity.

To conclude this chapter, while free will and determinism both can be seen as valid Christian theology, it is in works-based divine compensation theology in the context of free will and determinism that is completely and thoroughly discreditable theology, serving only to support religious intermediary schemes as outlined in Chapter Three. Trying to tabulate what is 'owed' from God, or seeking to either individually or collectively will divine favor is completely preposterous as Christian doctrine. Fatalism, not faith, has reared its head here. To foolishly live in this world solely for preparation of the afterlife, considered on the balance of good deeds is as faulty a line of reasoning as living by axiomatic indoctrination to strive toward ritualistic 'purity' as described in Chapter Three. Both are spiritually stunting faulty beliefs. Superstition, not faith is found where divine favor is thought possible to be willed through static and ritualized acts and offerings. Being an accountant of what would be sufficient payment to lay claim to something of 'spiritual worth' is but merely another form of cultish works-based behavior. It is another manifestation of the superstitious and obsessive-compulsive mindset based in the fear of uncertainty of the unknown. The only math minimally needed for one's spiritual preparation for physical end is perhaps to simply know there are two spiritual laws that guide free will: 1. Love God and 2. Love humanity.

In terms of free will, it can be simply reduced to the idea that one's own good nature *(after all, humanity was created from substance that can be thought of as compossible with God's goodness)* will have but a minimal impact on the will of God because good human nature is already built within and into human DNA, but sometimes it just needs to be sought and found within.

Why? Because God created you! He already knows all about you! Have faith in that! Find freedom in that! God created *you*! *He chose you* to be a desirable part His creation, and God creates from a place of goodness!

Therefore, no matter what you think of yourself or if you believe you have or have not earned divine favor, your spiritual well-being rest assured is going to be well cared for by God in His intended purpose. The only math needed is to simply be able count to two and remember to carry out activities in a way that is compatible with, and more to the point, not contrary to the greatest two Commandments.

To be consciously mindful to choose to do what is right, whether it will be pleasing to God or whether a person feels exclusively chosen to do so, is to freely fulfill the self spiritually. At the same time, to search for, and to discover what it is that has been predetermined by God's will for each individual is a sound and sensible exploratory journey to freely undertake and to seek to fulfill. Perhaps doing Right because it is Right to do so, and for the right reason alone, can also help to answer something of the why of the created universe, and why it is that human free will exists in the omniscience of God and His created universe.

Predestination? Yes! God already knows all about every person.

Free will? Yes! Selflessly choosing to make a difference for humanity is the Right thing to do.

Chapter 5

Enter Kurt Gödel: The Limitation of Logic is that Logic is Parametric

Problems with Seeking Finite Logical Coherence in an Infinite Universe

"Axiomatic truth is truth by declaration"

(Kryzanowski, 2024).

This ridiculous quotation as a stand-alone axiom, is of course self-referential, and can therefore be thought of as discreditable as absolute 'truth'.

In isolation, problems with the above statement include the absence of a point of comparison, a lack of any sort of further clarification, no examples to in any way support its validity, and in its isolation, there is no external way to verify properties of 'truth' it alleges to contain within its message.

While seemingly self-evident, the contents of the statement perhaps make it entirely plausible as a stand-alone claim, given that the practical application of the statement above, might, as a concept, have practical uses in some circumstances. Yet, as a statement in isolation, there are limitations therefore in its capacity to be provable. This is especially the case if the above axiom is prevented from interacting with other ideas. For example, to find out what the color green looks like, using deductive observation, a person must be able to know what green does not look like as a point of reference. For moral truth, as in, to know right from wrong, a person must know at least something of what is 'wrong' to understand what it is that is 'right'; and then how to act accordingly. In mathematical terms, it is much the same. Like the written word, without a system to distinguish one mathematical symbol from another, the individual becomes lost in a world of meaningless scratches and marks where there is no ability to compare and distinguish ones from others. Similarly, in the absence of spoken communication, in the absence of gestural references, or with no communication in any written, gestural or linguistic form, there can be no understanding or agreement among people as to the very nature and properties of 'truth' found contained within the ideas expressed in these ways.

While agreement among people as to what truth is does not necessarily make something truth, is truth something absolute as a universal property? As in, does it exist in the absence of ability to discern between ideas, or in the absence of common communication through which to compare understanding with others? Or is what is deemed truth more a function of human-made construction of agreements?

Trying to will truth into existence by consensus, like through repetitive messaging, or by sloganeering for example, is tantamount to trying to create, or to 'manufacture' truth (as could be expressed in modern and industrialized terms). If truth is something that contains within it properties of absolute universality, then truth does not require belief in it for it to be truth. Does truth require formation from meaning that is constructed from natural world perceptual inputs? Are observations and/or experiences truth-creating? Or do observations and experiences create understanding of truth? Or is the nature of 'truth' as an absolute universal property something quite different? If so, would it not require perception of it, would it not require experience with it (except perhaps to practice it), and would it not require agreement about what it is for it to exist as truth? If Truth is thought of as universal principle or property, Truth would simply exist whether it is known about, acknowledged, understood, or perceived or not.

The greatest logical tool a person has available to weigh and evaluate what constitutes 'truth' is the mind. To know something of the difference between a 'good' idea and a 'bad' idea, and to be equipped to discern between what is morally 'right' or 'wrong' is available through channels of intellectual methods for people who are willing to seek truth that way. The rich tradition of Greek, Roman, Hebrew, and Mediterranean scholarship prior to Jesus' time testifies to the merits of developing rational and intellectual understandings and philosophies. To understand what Truth is, and what is right or wrong the human mind requires a standard of truth and morality by which to compare words and deeds spoken or done by oneself, or the same by other people.

On this point, the Christian who lives by way of heart first, would benefit from backstopping their moral convictions of conscience with firm grounding in rigorous intellectual scholarship. This is lest they find their heart swayed by uncritically accepting false belief.

To understand properties and qualities of physical 'matter' of the universe (in this case, to understand 'truths' such that the physical 'reality' of the universe might have 'truth' contained within the properties of the substances and materials of the universe that substantiate their existence), the human mind gives people capacity to come to agreement or disagreement through intersubjective experience.

That is, the human mind takes in perceptions and draws conclusions about what it observes. That more than one person can independently verify and substantiate baseline reality to a large degree therefore helps create plausibility that physical and material 'truth' is independent from individual perception of it. For example, if two people walk into a room and see a chair in the middle of the room and can both agree that it is a chair, this helps to substantiate that there exists truth in object physical world reality independent of sole individual perception of it.

Further, if the two people who agree that what they saw was a chair are in agreement with two more people who enter at a later time, without being told there is a chair in the room, but enter, then agree there is a chair, and then are later able to declare they saw the same thing, this more so helps to substantiate physical reality as truly existing, and that there is truth in physical reality, independent of the influence of perception of it and on it. Again, though to simply agree with other people that something is truth does not make it so. While physical reality might be possible to verify as containing true properties, universal governing ideas, universal governing principles, and in particular, what is universally governing moral truth in the world are perhaps all more difficult to substantiate by intersubjective agreement alone.

To be able to independently substantiate universal 'reality' as a form of 'truth', for people to have the conscious wherewithal to contemplate that they themselves contain properties and concept of 'self', to be able to understand that other people are real, and equipped in much the same way, and therefore form part of reality as well, the human being is well- equipped with agency of mind (perhaps as from Chapter 4 citing the mind of Helen Keller proposing that the mind is external to physical-world reality is a proposition, if valid, that is of benefit for people to be able to externally evaluate what is to valid and true from falsehoods, where the mind is external to physical-world reality.

The degree to which creatures of the animal kingdom may have similar capabilities creates an interesting point of comparison and discussion. To the extent that other species can know something of natural world truth in the same way, or that they might vary in the degree to which they have capacity to know and understand these thing, points to properties unique to the human mind and its ability to use logic and other tools of perception and evaluation to understand and contemplate the nature of the real (physical) universe, but more-so to have capacity to understand what are perhaps less tangible but real universal principles of existence, morality and truth.

The agency of human mind has such tremendous capability whether God is accepted as a universal constancy, universal creator, or as the highest standard of morality, with Jesus as His example, or not. If it is found to be the case that on the balance, much of human free will is a function of mind, then proportionally, intersubjective agreement among people as to whether God exists or not does not matter, because God would not and does not require belief in His existence to exist.

For check and balance on the power of the rational human mind, the framework of Kurt Gödel's Incompleteness Theorems (1931), and drawn from them, the 'Paradox of Undecidability' have positive uses as part of the toolkit of mind for what is the entirely logical purpose of holding human understanding of logical stability and certainty under scrutiny. This with the intention to prevent holding what might be thought of as 'truths' for granted, or without questioning.

That the logic of the Incompleteness Theorems are themselves paradoxically a tool of logic, but critical of logic, is in itself an odd problem of self-reference in logical systems, but this itself opens doors of curiosity by suggesting that logic and systems of logic are not nearly as stable as is commonly and all too easily often accepted without question. As a system of logic understanding itself the theorems demonstrate ways in which logical approaches to understanding 'truths' can easily become muddled in self-contradiction, self-declared provability, and lacking complete system consistency.

The Incompleteness Theorems originally uncovered challenges in mathematical theory with fixed symbols and the operations of mathematics on its fixed symbols, and the degree to which such activities offer anything that is really provable, even if replicable.

If symbols and principles of mathematics are thought to be axioms of foundational universal property, rather than a way to explain universal properties, and as well, if mathematical principles lend themselves to being used as tools of operative procedures and functions, to be performed upon mathematical objects, for example, organizing sets of symbols and then performing various operations, procedures, or functions like addition, subtraction, multiplication, or division using organized sets of symbols, for mathematics to demonstrate consistency and coherence, the breakdown of mathematical thinking as a form of logical understanding, it will be proposed in this Chapter will likely crack, crumble, or perhaps, even as the book title somewhat audaciously suggests, might possibly destruct from within the logical systems themselves. This when logical systems are at their boundaries of function, purpose, or unknowing of totality or consistency.

By putting processes of logical formalism from various spheres of human understanding under scrutiny using the Incompleteness Theorems, including mathematical and scientific logical systems, political linguistic and rhetorical logical systems, and the logic of intellectualized systems of moral understanding, this chapter will test the degree to which these logical 'systems' of thinking succumb to internal tension contained within their own enclosures of axioms (symbols and properties within parameters) and within the way the sets of symbols axiomatic to the particular systems are limited and pressured by operations put onto the systems' own self-defined closed loop parameters, and the way in which 'undecidable' external factors can inevitably destabilize what are thought to be complete sets and systems, when undecidability is inserted into them. For example, if mathematical logic can be thought of as a system of collecting symbols together, ordering them, and binding them into sets, and by doing so, having restricted the set of symbols as best as possible by finite parameters, in order to say, perform operations such as testing a set of axioms for consistency, or to test an axiom for something of containing properties of validity, or even 'truth' (by measuring it, comparing it, or inserting variability into its parameters and onto the set to see what happens), this type of understanding will be argued to contain incompleteness and limit as a way understanding by its own definition and purpose to create limitations. Seeing the world solely in this limited and minimal way for minds tilted toward seeking spiritual understanding, it becomes apparent that relying solely on tangible and finite practical and logical understandings cannot reasonably offer full understanding, nor even do they fully provide rich enough experiences of human knowing.

Efforts to demonstrate that logical reasoning, formal scientific methods, and rationalism either are, or ought to be guiding thought processes, and even as a mandate or idealized ethos of intellectual scholarship, while incredibly valuable, will be made to show there is more instability at the level of this kind of foundational human acquired knowledge, than many people seem to believe.

To the staunchest of believers in the triumph of logical understanding as absolute and complete in the face of spiritualist arguments to the contrary, this chapter may hopefully induce something of an existential crisis and internal examination in people who hold steadfast in belief to the gospel of science as salvation. The idea that logic and spirituality are separate encampments, as though there is an absolute split between rationalism and spiritualism, will be more clearly shown in this chapter to not be optimal or even helpful for understanding the physical nature of the 'real' universe to begin with. As well, for people yet undecided, to demonstrate that universal intangibilities of understanding morality and the nature of what Truth is, will be shown to be limited when approached solely from rational intellect. If a person chooses to seek deeper understanding than rationalism alone can provide, perhaps it might be helpful to use rationalism to first internally clarify personal spiritual belief about God, but also to recognize that reason alone has limits. To know that it is okay to put faith to the good where logical limits of knowing reach their limits can offer assurances of an intangible nature where logic and reason can offer only tangible certainty, which is a limited kind of assurance of well-being because people live in a finite physical world existence.

Separation of church and state has been demonstrated to be of tremendous benefit for society for this purpose. Between material well-being and spiritual well-being, the latter has often become ignored despite the potential for reciprocity between both often going unnoticed. However, despite the benefits, detachment from spiritual engagement has been an unintended consequence of separation of church involvement in state affairs. The remedy in this situation is not to reinsert the church into state affairs, but instead is for individuals to simply recover and reclaim their spiritual self.

Freedom of conscience in the 21st century has morphed, has become quite distorted, and has quite become grotesque in its manifestation and realization in its current form. A basic example of free will as a distorted concept can be seen, for example, in subtle changes in language use, and how its differing use comes to suit particular situations where differing uses are convenient or favorable, but not necessarily accurate or precise. For example, language drift in popular media has made acceptable discourse validating the use of expressions such as 'my truth' and 'your truth', supplanting language of 'my opinion' and 'your opinion' is troublesome in this regard. Who can respectfully disagree, argue respectfully with, or argue even without being elevated in language and emotion, when a claimed absolute idea such as: 'my truth' (closed loop in its self-declarative authority) is deployed on issues or in circumstances arising where such language limits discourse on problems in common with the people involved? Basic agreement on facts would offer something of a minimum baseline of what something of 'truth' is when dubious terminology like 'my truth' and 'your truth' are invoked. For people who speak this way, absent is the realization that truth is not creatable, and to claim it as 'one's own' does not support the pursuit of truth. This is because absolute truth would have no owner. Declarative claims to absolute truth further put the onus on the self-declared 'owner' to such claims to present their case for proof of titled ownership of said 'truths'. If there is a claim of ownership of 'my truth' or 'your truth' this should not be a conversation ending, but instead, ought to be subjectable to extra scrutiny, validation of claim, or, if not provided, then the claim ought to be ignored or laughed off as discreditable.

Considering the divorce of spiritual and rational philosophy that has left many people in the 21st century adrift and confused, that Kurt Gödel's Incompleteness Theorems exist as a tool of logical rationalism demonstrating the limits of logical rationalism, is seemingly quite odd, and perhaps appear as further confoundment, but will be shown to be transferable from the realm of understanding mathematical limits, to those of philosophy and the use of rhetorical language as well. The Incompleteness Theorems provide an opportunity to challenge acceptance of logical formalism as the supreme authority in human understanding.

In the passage of time of approximately two-thousand years since the life and teachings of Christ overturned the fallacy of relying solely on intellectualism as the most advanced form of human thought and governance of interaction, it can perhaps be seen that instead a bridge of reciprocity between rationalism and spiritualism freely open and as a back and forth channel, can stimulate and enhance gains made in both ways of understanding, and open a door for the 21st century person to reclaim their spiritual self.

Experimentation with the Limits of Logic in Political Discourse

Politics is particularly well known for its appeal to emotional sentiment as well as for its use of 'logic' and 'reason' to develop laws, contracts, agreements, declarations, treaties, alliances, pacts, declarations of war, and many articles of governance by which and under which people around the world might become beholden to or bound. For this reason, it is important to understand the logic of politics, its pitfalls, and its limits.

The sphere of political logic and its built-in lever of world authority and power are often used as way by which people and groups of all sorts seek to attain the legitimacy of governing status (attained justifiably or not). Politics contains within its system of logical procedure and expression the backstop of heavy-handed enforcement of decisions and resolutions that are made by its mechanisms. Also, principles of political logic have a significant effect on, and influence over the world and its people, and the direction of societies during the course of history and life (in both good and bad ways). For these reasons, the sphere of political logic will make for an excellent yet simple place to experiment with axioms and how they interact with formal logic systems as a process. Even if a political process is highly consistent, and even if the axioms of political rhetoric within the system are thought to be sound, this section will demonstrate that in its ideological world of often questionable '-isms' and causes, the political sphere most often leaves participants feeling incomplete when higher purpose or sense of belonging is sought from this source.

The built-in tension between 'rational' vs. emotive contrastive rhetoric found inherent in political discourse renders its logical foundation perhaps 'self-evidently' unstable or perhaps 'quite obviously' unstable to many people who are politically enthusiastic or even zealous in this regard. Yet, many people who declare their awareness of such problems found within political logic, its coherence (or lack thereof), will often become seduced into professing political dogma as 'truth' despite this awareness. For example, perhaps there are times where political alliance is thought to be of greater immediate concern and this belief will override a person's own conscience or personal contrary belief system. Another example of this phenomena might be where personal internal political belief turns to prescriptive moral grandstanding, and then coincides with a mandate for political ideology to be held in higher regard than people themselves. For a final example of rationalist vs. emotive tension that might be found in political discourse, is the human desire to be fulfilled by a sense of community in something believed to offer meaning greater than personal interest. Political dogma often easily offers promise to fulfill such needs.

As with any logical concept, for a political idea to be considered truthful, or at least minimally provable, it cannot refer to itself as truth. Declarative truisms can be expressed by way of written language among other ways. A linguistic example can be found in the silly declarative axiom at the beginning of the preamble to this chapter: *"axiomatic truth is truth by declaration"*. When the content is stripped from the statement, the functions of the content reveal the metalanguage of the statement. At this level, the axiom at the beginning of the chapter can be exposed by its own idiocy: *"x is x because x says it is"*. Now, instead of converting the axiom back into its original state, as an experiment, substituting x for another subject, and then modifying the phraseology for effect produces another wonderfully pseudo-profound declaration: *"A parrot is a parrot because it calls itself one."*

Truth is often thought to be present and with greater clarity when mathematical symbols are used to try and express it. Perhaps there is an unspoken assumption that written mathematical expressions of ideas somehow offer greater assurance that what is said is truthful. Nonetheless, however an idea is expressed, whether by using linguistic or mathematical symbols, self-reference contained within declarative statements lack provability, and are therefore undecidable as 'truth', as per Gödel's 2nd Incompleteness Theorem (Crilly, 2011, p. 189). For the human mind to fully understand declarative ideas, it requires a point of comparison or referent. Please see the supplemental practical material at the back of this volume for more context, also, please consult the back matter for further reading regarding problems of logic in both language and mathematics.

At least even minimally, if a declaration is to be considered 'valid', in the absence of any external point of reference, even if the internal logic of the statement is somehow consistent, it cannot be certain that it will be completely consistently free from contradiction across all situations. This is because it cannot be possible to observe all possible situations (Crilly, 2011, p. 189). For example, under the "x is x because it says it is" formula, the parrot might say *"I'm a parrot"* in one situation and then say *"I'm a toucan"* in another situation not subsequently witnessed.

Again, the idea of universal validity is not approachable as a declarative concept under the limits of such expressions of logic. The Incompleteness Theorems call into question the validity of mathematical 'objects' (axioms) and their representation by mathematical symbols, as though symbols contain understood absolute form. By extension, formal procedures (operations) of manipulation of symbols are exposed as limited in their ability to reveal anything of greater meaning than the attributes the symbols are associated with, or the meaning they are thought to hold within them.

The Incompleteness Theorems cannot assess the interaction between human cognitive perception of physical world sets and intent to order physical world sets in comparison to the degree to which ordered sets and logical systems are part of physical world reality independent of observation perception. This adds another layer of complication when trying to understand particularly whether there are universal principles of truth.

If any universal properties of mathematics, universal properties of the physical world, or universal principles of philosophy or theology exist and contain absolute truth, is it that the human ability to fully understand limited by cognitive capacities, or are limitations presented in the universalities more-so related to a lack of absolutism in properties and principles of the universe? Before considering this question in the context of political logic further, it will be helpful to deeply consider some core questions that the fallacy of truth by declaration brings out.

To approach anything of absolute truth (if political logic could ever plausibly offer or provide such a thing), questions of importance for consideration are whether truth is something that truth requires perception of it, meaning is truth contained only in interaction between people ~ world, people ~ people? Or does truth exist independently of whether it can be observed, experienced, or agreed upon or not? If something is truth, doesn't it mean, that to know it as truth, it must have a point of reference? That is, to distinguish principles of truth from what is not, then there must be error. However, if every object that exists is true in that it is part of reality, then there must be something external to the universe that can observe its object truth and its existence. The nature of what is considered truth, or what is even to be considered real can be elusive from within the parameters of natural world reality itself. Because people reside within the parameters of the physical world and because human ability to fully know what truth is within it (like any tangible kind of understanding) actually requires an external point of reference to assess validity. Problems of interpretation of object reality and physical world phenomena arise because the natural world cannot wholly be observed without human interaction as part of it and influencing it. If any kind of truth, including absolute universal properties and principles can be known intellectually, then perhaps it is a strength to further consider whether the human mind is external to physical world reality rather than emergent from it. The elusive question of where the mind resides ought to be explored further in various fields of study because it would be beneficial to help understand universal truth where the mind might not actually tangibly or wholly reside within the physical brain. This would be important further to explore not only properties and principles of universal truth separately, but to explore *interactions between* properties and principles of universal truth additionally.

For the agnostic, atheist, humanist, religious, spiritual, or otherwise inclined person, if it there is hope for at least one kind of universal truth to be unified under, then hopefully, it would at least be moral truth for people to be less barbarous and less destructive. For the logical aspect of the human mind to understand properties and principles of universal truth, to be equipped with an impartial toolkit, perhaps to accept that the human mind is not necessarily completely axiomatic to natural world reality itself would be helpful.

To view moral truth as universal constancy, hopefully will close the door to lines of reasoning that seek to give credibility to ideas that moral truth is merely a relative concept, or one based on agreements between and among people (especially where people with political motivation and clout are moral relativists). What problems would arise if the nature of moral truth was limited by relativism? Opening up the history book of human political conduct and affairs answers that question quite well. The importance of calling political logic into question at its foundations is of great importance as an expression of human morality, whether taken from a philosophical or theological standpoint, because of the influence and political pressure that is put upon humanity by political powers.

Axiomatic Political Logic and Its Problems in Microcosm

How often in casual conversations among people are familiar axioms tossed around carelessly yet definitively?

For example:

- 'That's just how it is.'
- 'You only live once (YOLO).'
- 'It is what it is.'
- 'We are all in this together.'
- 'Live fast and die hard.'
- 'The rich get richer; the poor get poorer.'
- 'What doesn't kill you makes you stronger.'
- 'Time heals all wounds.'
- 'Birds of a feather flock together.'
- 'Opposites attract.'
- 'You can't teach an old dog new tricks.'
- 'It's a long shot.'
- 'Keeping it real.'
- 'Surviving.'
- ''Too chill for that.'
- 'Stay strong.'
- 'Hang in there.'
- 'You've got to keep on keeping on.'
- 'Take things one day at a time.'

- 'Live day to day.'
- 'Every cloud has its silver lining.'
- 'A dollar saved is a dollar earned.'

The above list is a small, paraphrased sampling of frequently used uncritical linguistic axioms in circulation at the time and place of writing. Surveying this list, several things stand out in terms of commonality among the phrases, their axiomatic properties, and the ethical principles underlying them. For example, the above list of axioms summarizes what might otherwise be nuanced experiences of life into simplistic ways to explain such experiences. Another commonality can be observed in their reference to hardship. A third commonality implied from within these axioms is insistence on attending to matters of hardship with a sense of immediacy. Fourth, underlying their usage is a short-term outlook emphasizing a singular next-step action. As a final identifiable commonality they share is a restrictive mindset that underwrites the sentiment carried by these axiomatic phrases.

Whether it is restriction contained within the axioms suggested for another person to abide by, or whether the axiom is to be taken as a remedy to fix the underlying sentiment proposed inferentially by these kinds of phrases, there is a problem underlying this type of phraseology and by association, this type of thought. That is, they all lean toward a certain 'endure to survive' attitude expressed or implied within them. For example, to suggest to someone to 'take things day by day' implies necessity to just withstand hardship from one period to the next. Or for someone to choose to act with reckless largess at the suggestion of such axioms as: 'You only live once, right?' implies that because the future is uncertain then to exist solely for what is happening in the right now is the optimal way to be. Or when asking how someone is doing, by responding: 'I'm surviving, is it the weekend yet?' is another phrase referencing toil in one's work and restriction of time in which to actually seek enjoyment or rest.

Understanding that many of these types of linguistic axioms might simply occur as a function of being made 'in passing', or while 'on the go', like in a workplace for example, nonetheless, the consistent metalanguage of this sample set of idiomatic phrases contains in common an underlying fixed and rigid way of expressing how to endure restriction and hardship, often with implied immediacy. When the use of phrases like these (and when stronger phrases of limitation or restrictive mindset are used) they can become ingrained into the character of people who regularly think, say, and ultimately live out the kind of harsh lifestyle many of these axioms prescribe. The underlying attitude derived from the rhetoric of these phrases also becomes a kind of social currency, medium of exchange, or vetting tool among people who subscribe to the political ethic of hard-done-by-ism.

For political opportunists, onset hard-done-by-ism makes easy bait of people who practice its doctrine of victimhood and misery. This is a deep problem that can emerge where such mindset takes hold. Meaning that from within the mindset of people who tilt their words to expression of axioms of hard-done-by-ism, the quality of their actions results in degraded (spiritual and economic) well-being stuck within their fixed 'endure and survive' the 'right nowness' of life mindset. Unfortunately for people who think like this, there are any number of charismatic politicians waiting to affirm and to validate their hard-done-by, woe-is-me attitude, ready to make the empty promise of "jam tomorrow" made by the White Queen to Alice in Through the Looking Glass by Lewis Carroll (1871).

Problems of society can spiral further downward when they are built on a foundation of short-term thinking and negativity as expressed in the axiomatics above.

The rigidity of axiom shows its weakness here as a perpetual and even 'contagious' thought habit of individuals and societies. To further address the limits of logical validity of political rhetoric and breakdown of logic in the political sphere, is to point out the reflexive and off-the-cuff usage and proliferation of these types of axioms. Sadly, they often can and do become very deeply ingrained into the customs and social currency of people and societies where these terms are regularly deployed. The consequence to the downside is one of stagnation and decline in wellness and prosperity in people who parrot the ethos held by fixed and restrictive axiom. Further to this, the tension between reasonability and emotion in political rhetoric swings toward negative sentiment and fervor in the doctrine of hard-done-by-ism. This kind of ethos can drive down the climate of a workplace where excessive expressions of these kinds of sentiments create an excessively negative work-site custom of social culture.

At another level of deepening consequence, when such axioms become so overused or so completely entrenched into the societal mindset, they, or others like them, might begin to drift from an expression of negative sentiment only into the realm of fixed ideology. The prospect of negative sentiment found in these kinds of axioms can gain momentum, and then very quickly the axiom, then sentiment, then ideology, then becomes a movement call toward action. Unfortunately, from this tailspin, hard-done-by-ist believers reintroduce their fixed axioms, but now, they are presented in the form of woe-is-me bullet-phrase sloganeering or propaganda. Embedded in the mindset of survivalism comes expression of urgency in the actions necessary to rectify the perceived harm and affliction expressed from the original axioms, as they become agreed upon truth as indicative of inflicted hardship. Fervor and zealotry may take hold as calls of higher purpose are invoked through the validity of the axiom as being a call to action. By extension, further problems arise when axiomation become further galvanized into unquestionable dogmatism.

To help discredit the notion of 'higher purpose' that might be invoked through political mandate by axiom, the list of axioms of hardship presented earlier will be mechanically drawn from, to breakdown claims to absolute truth their sentiment might believe to contain. Dubious politics and maligned persuasion drawn from the rhetoric that might be invoked or might emerge from the list of hard-done-by axioms from above will be intentionally concocted here, for use as a method of analysis and as an example of how to refute political dogma and action from dogma that people might otherwise undertake to find something of spiritual or social belonging or connectedness in their practice.

The method of concoction is to take the list above as a 'menu' of options from which to create a vacuous and meaningless 'call to action'. Several of the selected axioms from the set will be ordered into a string of dialogue of logical progression. It will be proposed that depending on how such a dialogue is presented in isolation to an external observer, the dialogue might be thought to contain coherent meaning that is seen to exist between the chain of selected axioms, even though they have been somewhat arbitrarily strung together. Within the selected axioms presented in dialogue below, the emergence of a fabricated but seemingly internally consistent and coherent dialogue containing politicized discussion will be created. It will have emerged simply by way of having ordered a selection of thoughtless axioms, now ideologically charged, and depending on the tone in which the dialogue could be read; the dialogue might take on the character of an urgent call to political action, especially if they can be imagined to be possibly extended and broadened into larger proportions in society.

From simply drawing from the menu of pre-selected axioms of declarative restriction and woe-is-me-ism, a hypothetical proposal to act politically on their foundation can been made. The narrative of hardship contained in each axiom and extended along the string of hypothetical conversation reinforcing each previous one will demonstrate in microcosm the potential contained within for people with such mindsets of axiom to become politically charged and to move (with fervor) toward action to 'right' whatever the burning issue might be. Perhaps as a chat among like-minded friends or co-workers, (once again arbitrarily strung together as a list of pre-selected dogmatic axioms), the dialogue could be peppered with varying phrasing and tone. Tired metalanguage in the dialogue below creates a contrived hypothetical grievance:

Bill: *"The rich keep getting richer!"*

Frank: *"For sure, and the poor, well, they keep getting poorer!"*

Bob: *"Yeah, that's how it is alright!"*

Frank: *"I agree with you, birds of a feather! We are all in this together!"*

Bill: *"Well, yeah, you only live once, so we might as well live fast and die-hard!"*

These are simplistic, silly, uncritical, and seemingly innocuous axioms, peppered with everyday phraseology, and used very often every day in social interactions in the present time and place. Yet, they have been composed in such a way that, perhaps from the underlying mindset of restriction and hard-done-by ethos of limitation, there could emerge something of an ideology and a call to action from the sentiments they echo. Thinking about the bullet-like 'truth' each one of these micro-messages might contain within it, perhaps, the move from social banter to a call to political action might not be too far of a leap. Would these axioms or ones like them not make excellent fodder for sloganeering to be written onto signs for political messaging? Would these axioms, when sloganeered and infused into various forms of media and methods of communication, electronic or otherwise, perhaps have the potential to speak to and capture the imagination and agency of people in a place of life whereby they might be receptive to a call to action this way? If the script was read out loud, and read with varying degrees of tone, urgency or fervor, or, if the phrasings were presented with elevated gradations of rigid or inflammatory language, the inclinations for people who are primed toward seeking meaning and purpose through the political 'isms' of the world might become very receptive to political mobilization.

Notice at this point that no specific cause or problem has been asserted or proposed in the dialogue above. If Bill, Bob, and Frank are colleagues in a place of work, the conversation might have been part of an ongoing discussion around wages. Such axioms, or ones like them, could quite easily be shouted into a megaphone as bullets of truth, composed into a mantra and then repeated as a chant. As though repeating them at louder and louder volumes will somehow make the axioms or string of them become 'true' through such activity. This scenario might become more ridiculous further if the premise of claims to hardship are not really valid. The inflexibility of 'truth by axiom' shows its problems, tremendous weaknesses, and even potential for harm when used as a tool of charged politicism. For example, the original statement in the set of axioms of the 'rich get richer' is likely agreed on by premise by the men as a problem requiring resolution. If the rest of the conversation continues uncritically and unquestioningly along the lines of undue hardship, it might make sense to these men for their line of axiomatic reasoning to become a call to action for higher wages. If the 'rich' do 'in fact' get 'richer' is accepted as an ingrained 'truth' from the outset, and is accepted as a moral 'wrong' that needs 'righted' (and as it is a well-known point of heated contention in current times), this line of thinking is frequently used in the context of speaking about matters of money and what might constitute 'just compensation' ('Fair Wages for All!').

If considered at yet another level deeper, perhaps the problem is more in poverty of the fixed, rigid, and inflexible mindsets of the fictitious Bill, Bob, and Frank. None of the gentlemen involved have bothered to find out if their premise is valid. For example, embedded in the axiom of the 'rich get richer and poor get poorer' is the assumption that to be 'rich' (speaking solely in monetary terms), is a fixed way of being. Or that 'the rich' are somehow a static body of people. Similarly, the three men have a fixed perception regarding the condition of people who they deem to be statically 'poor'. The men have bonded together in their perception of misery and subsequent agreement about the 'truth' of 'how it is' (whatever that means). Perhaps they are disenfranchised or dissatisfied with their personal situations, which likely tilt toward being less financially well-off. Yet, in this conversational snapshot, they have neglected and denied themselves any prospect or potential for self-generated upward economic mobility. To them, the problem of being underpaid has been thrust upon them externally.

Hopefully, people who are inclined to think this way will find comfort and solace bonding over the social currency of this sort of shared woe-is-me-ism. This kind of axiomation of thought fabricated above from a pre-selected menu, represents the kind of sloganeering that perhaps encapsulates the essence and expression of the sort of social cohesion and belonging found in political propaganda and through participating in the '-isms' of shared higher moral purpose borne from perceived political 'injustice' or 'deficit': *"Wrongdoing! Hardship! Urgency! Action!"*

If Frank got a promotion, or finds a way to improve his financial situation, perhaps he will be met with social ostracization from Bill and Bob from their lack of success in the same way. Harmful political ideologies seem to spring quite easily from restrictive and rigid habits of pessimistic thought, including envy especially. The idea of political axiom as 'truth' (well over-used, and quite easily scientifically systemized into sloganeering, coercion, and propaganda) as a political call to action, it is often particularly persuasive when used to gain and bolster political support from people with such mindsets of hardship. Often the mindset of hardship originates in felt unjust affliction in the political and economic sense (rightly or wrongly). Some sort of rectification of the situation must be reconciled by people who are thought to be externally responsible for the wrongdoing. Most often however, people who are motivated by such systems of political belief seek to make the situation 'right' by extraction of resources acquired by people who have sought economic self-improvement, and have succeeded in doing so within the same political and economic framework of society shared with people claiming woe-is-me-ism.

Christian political propagandists operate in much the same way when scripture is turned into axiom, and then twisted into political dogma similarly. Taking scripture pericopes and then turning them into bullet-messages lends well to sloganeering and propaganda similarly: *"Ye Must Be Born Again!"* comes to mind as an immediate example. It is as though in bullet form; people who choose this kind of religious expression believe they can summarize the Christian message into simple axiom and then create the same sense of urgency and call to immediate action. For example, it is not uncommon to walk down the street and encounter people from various organizations under the banner of "Christianity" to be found with tables set up full of pamphlets and literature shouting into megaphones. To call people to urgent and immediate action regarding the state of their soul with a megaphone to their lips using the scripture passages that lend themselves well to bullet point sloganeering become thrust onto the public. At times, this kind of 'evangelism' might be peppered with overtones of judgment put on the people subjected to this version Christianity, while they simply pass by on the street. Oblivious to the street preacher of this kind, is that people passing by might find it off-putting to receive something of what Christian life might be like if this kind of street preacher is their first example, and if the 'Christian' message they are subjected to is one full of distortion and is a rather grotesque expression of abject doom and hopelessness.

Blasting out dogma in the name of Christianity through the doctrine of fear, the street preachers who do so are seemingly oblivious to their own discrediting. Trying to motivate people by fear to accept the Christian message by threatening imminent doom and coming hellfire is not quite as effective a tool of evangelism as such people might think it to be. That personal spiritual development might take longer than the time of a quick intrusive encounter to fully arrive, and that the slow approach to becoming aware of, and understanding the spiritual self will likely result in a more authentic spiritual formation does not seem to be held in high regard by this kind of messenger.

Like in the religious example above, the practitioners of the political '-isms' of the world often claim that such doom is imminent and under the impetus of 'act now'. This urgency of course, if acted upon, strips the would-be prospect of their own critical lens of contemplation and spiritual development by jumping into 'the cause' without a second sober second thought. In this regard, the commercial axiom of: 'Act now before the sale ends!' comes to mind. Whether through initial waiver of personal agency, or of a longing perhaps to find 'acceptance', or whether through worn-down and repeated coercion while affiliated with such a political or religious organization, the logic of: 'wrongdoing

-hardship -urgency - action' can be applied as a tool of analysis, when trying to understand various political and religious movements, and what to expect if a person chooses to join their cause.

If such dogma is explicit at the outset of introduction to the organization, once further involved with the group, then when the layers of the onion become peeled back further it will likely reveal deeper levels of coercion and surrender of personal agency upon further involvement. If a person accepts simple axioms as absolute truth, the person primed to express themselves in such absolutes, is conveying elements of reductionism and restriction in their internal mindset. The person who might be seeking certainty, order, and constancy may certainly find some elements of those by joining such political movements. However, have they found 'truth'? The conscript might come to resent the surrender of their own free agency to the 'higher purpose' of the 'greater good' when they come to discover that at the outset, the premise of the political movement was on shaky ground.

There might be logical 'coherence' as described above, in the set of axioms, or in the articles of belief and the mandates of the group. The principles of each article of axiom within the self-contained set of logical 'truisms' might continue from its premise along something of a continuum of logical process. However, with a lack of external verification of the validity of the axiomatics within a political movement, even if there is something of importance or even 'truth' in the political '-ism' of the group (and perhaps there may very well be), even if the axioms agreed upon among the group members are viewed as 'truth', but if access is to externally referential material is limited or inhibited, then this raises any number of red flags.

At the point of breakdown and logical uncertainty in the movement's progress and procedures, was the faith the believer had in the original premise of the movement on solid ground? Was the original premise of the system of belief itself on solid ground such that a person will continue to be fulfilled in choosing to freely direct their efforts to it when the logic of the movement falters? Or will the believers in the political '-ism' require the lever of force to be thrust upon them to remain 'faithful' to the movement?

If Bob, Bill, and Frank believe their convictions have merit, and seek action based on the premise of their communally perceived economic hardship, they might very well gain support and find agreement from other people who are like-minded. On this point, they might very well find something of external validation of their premise of hardship. Further to this, they might find some success and validation through fulfilling their quest to achieve economic advancement and upward mobility from their doctrine of hardship.

However, none of this is the same as saying their declaration of hardship and doctrine of action to rectify their situation is, in the absolute, based in anyway upon a foundation of absolute 'truth'. It is not that the three men were even necessarily seeking to express any concept of absolute 'truth' in their aspirations, much more plainly and simply, in this hypothetical situation, they were likely simply just seeking a pay raise. The hopes that the pay raise would somehow fulfill their monetary hardships going forward may have been resolved upon implementing their call to action, or maybe not. However, if the outcome from their efforts to seek economic improvement did result in a pay rise, and they were satisfied that they had received the 'just compensation' they were seeking, the raise in pay will not in itself necessarily provide or guarantee the comfort of assurance and material improvement to their economic situations. This might be a function of their prior monetary habits that underscore their perceived hardship.

Perhaps it was the case that those problems were not even necessarily discussed thoroughly among each other, even contemplated from within themselves, or in honesty, perhaps their financial problems were not thoroughly discussed within their relationships. Within their families the financial problems might not have been discussed nor even have been transparent. If Bill enjoys a habit of online sports betting for example, that might very likely be more of an obstruction to his economic mobility and outcome than his rise in wages will provide for his family and himself. It is very likely that attaining more money will not fill the void he is experiencing in his life and seeking to fulfill through online betting. As for Bob, perhaps, his situation was not as dire as Bill, and maybe he was simply more interested in the comradery he found with his colleagues, or perhaps he has an overarching interest in the well-being of working people in the broader sense. If Frank took the promotion and found fulfillment that way, as well as receiving an accompanying raise in pay, perhaps he would have found something of what he was looking for that way.

For New Testament parables that are relatable to the hypothetical situation presented above of Bob, Bill, and Frank above please see:

Matthew 25: 14-30 and **Luke 19: 11-27**

For relatable context in early Greek philosophy and logic please see:

Aristotle: The Art of Rhetoric (ca. 4th century B.C.E.)

Experimentation with the Limits of Logic in 'Hard' Science: Is the Universe Parametrically Bound? Or is the Universe Infinitely Expanding?

Whether in the field of mathematics, science, moral philosophy, physics, religion, or any other, to seek truth by axiom is the same as the quest for universal constants across all situations. For an axiom to be universally true, it must be able to withstand all scrutiny. Yet, how long would it take to find out if an axiom is universally true? Is an axiom true across the vastness of the universe itself, or can an axiom even be universally true? For example, would 4+4 consistently be equal to 8 in all parts of the universe? Do lead, silver, or bromine for example, change in terms of their elemental physical composition in yet unknown regions of space? How would humans really be able to know? How do sound waves function in yet explored or not yet understood regions of the universe? Are physicists agreed that the speed of light is indeed a universal constant?

If light was found to be a universal constant in the way it functions as part of the universe, or for that matter, if lead, silver, or bromine are constant in the same manner consistent in property and character, does that imply that those elements are universally constant and then can be declared real as an axiomatic and unchanging feature of the universe? By extension, is it possible to say that constant properties of the universe can be considered to be 'true' if they are considered unchanging and real? Would universal constants then contain within them 'Truth'? In some way can universal constants contain elements of Truth or can something of universal Truth be learned from them in short human existence? If, in their universal constancy some physical properties of the universe are as old as the universe itself, can physical universal constants then declaratively be considered as such to be axioms, not only in universal property, but in universal principle also? On this point, perhaps it is more a case of semantic distinction.

If it is possible for people to have full and complete (plenary) knowledge of the physical universe, Gödel's Incompleteness Theorems would be resolved. Despite not being able to explain or understand universal 'why', in terms of advantage of mindset and outlook, research conducted by rationalist scientists demonstrates quite a distinct advantage and it can be acknowledged that they lead the way in their method of furthering human understanding in the realm of physical properties of the nature and reality of the universe, and as applicable to physical health and well-being. This is likely self-evident to most people in the 21st century, and it would be wise of course for religious zealots and even moderate theologians to readily concede this point. It might be again wise, as proposed in the introduction of this book for theologians to shift biblical research and writing away from assuming paradoxical problems are simply ones of unresolvable mystery. Also, for theologians or religious philosophers to refrain from shrouding paradoxical problems in the language of inexplicability, to explain away unrevealed or unrevealable phenomenon simply as mystery would be of tremendous benefit and appeal to many people who shy away from engaging with spiritual thought. Analogous to shifting away from liturgical Latin to vernacular languages in Church, this would be helpful to attract agnostics and skeptics to seek engagement with understanding of the Christian message and by extension for them to grow in their own spiritual well-being.

If this is a receptive message to 21st century theologians, that theologians would benefit from embracing advancements in scientific method and new discoveries in physics for example, might hopefully be heard because it creates an opportunity for well-educated yet spiritually adrift people to understand the Christian message and to include themselves as participants in Christian spiritual life.

Opening the discussion and study of biblical paradoxes and inconsistencies to a mindset of incompleteness in human knowledge, citing limited human capacity of mind for understanding the infinite knowledge contained and generated from the mind of an omniscient Creator, is not a proposal to abandon or relax the idea of faith, but rather, it is to have faith that the Christian message will hold its own because of human limitations by comparison.

These might be harsh words to hear perhaps for many people with deeply held convictions of faith. Perhaps, these are not even necessary words as a message for people with deeply held convictions of faith. As mentioned however, as will be seen in this section, formal logic has a parametric problem. This means that once a barrier or threshold of logical reasoning and ability is surpassed, or an unresolved theorem of some sort gets resolved, the parameter around the resolved logical problem has been surpassed, yet at the same time, it is simply the case that a new and expanded level of understanding reached is yet contained by more parameters. This phenomenon can be thought of as being very much analogous to dismantling and assembling a matryoshka doll and finding more dolls contained within, or similarly, adding more dolls outside of it, demonstrating the idea of infinite expansion and/or contraction.

Under the demonstrated success of Christian thought in the marketplace of spiritual ideas foremost, then why not in more general and perhaps in even more competitive marketplaces of ideas, why not subject the Christian message to the rigorous scrutiny of science in the same way? On the premise that Christian thought is freely available and offered by God for humanity to accept, there isn't really any existential threat to Christian thought at all, even if it is put under a broad range of intense scrutiny. As much as humanity enthusiastically loves and benefits from a scientific understanding of the world, it is the case that in contrast to God's love, scientific understanding and logical reasoning cannot love humanity in return. Nor can rationalism really explain or describe what it is like to experience God's love or can it explain human love for each other, other than by describing literal physiological responses and reactions. At the same time, science takes a double blow at human love, by tending to ignore the idea and study of the human spirit and the necessity of human spiritual nourishment and fulfillment. By God's offer of love, that it will always be freely available to all who seek to accept it, the theologian who feels some loss of faith in the Christian message due to scientific advancement can rest assured that God's love holds its own in any age.

However, as a warning to people (religious or otherwise), who may hold to such extreme and harmful concepts as 'faith healing' in the literal and physical sense, perhaps it is best for people who claim to be capable of such skills to put them to rest. The false hope and potential for medical harm toward others due to absence of intellectual understanding of functions of the human body, the faith-healer who insists upon the benefits of such false-health schemes has too directly conflated the practice of medicine in the scientific sense with the practice of wellness through spiritual health.

To consider becoming a member of an organization that practices faith-healing, alarm bells ought to go off if this is part of their doctrinal beliefs, because the organization is offering a false doctrine containing biblical non-essentialism to their adherents and subscribers. If the member of such a group is required to forgo personal medical autonomy as a condition of membership in the organization, the result is infringement and loss of personal agency in forgone legal rights where ideology becomes favored over people. The same might be said when politics and medicine become too comfortable resulting in the favorability of medical ideology derived from political rhetoric being held in higher regard than the actual health and medical well-being of the individual.

To put measured trust into a physician, licensed to practice medicine, that is, a person with deep and nuanced intellectual understanding of the operations of the human body, and who has experience with functions and qualities of it, including how to keep it running well and in an objectively healthy way, contrasted by a charlatan who believes they have 'preordained' power or claims to have been granted 'divine authority' to heal by trusting in them, shows the glaring simplistic absurdity of the latter type of 'medical' practice.

To profess to have the power to simply place a hand on someone who is ill or infirmed and by claiming capability to directly and literally cure illness, and then, to declaratively claim the illness has passed, citing higher powers at work through him, the faith 'healer', by freely chosen misuse of his hands and his words has professed to have willed an act of incompossibility. Chapter Four addressed the likelihood that a person can complete an act that is incompossible with the understood physical laws of nature as are currently known. Additionally, Chapter Three explored the harmful effects that dubious claims made by 'spiritual intermediaries' and those who offer 'special' divine insight offer to their clientele can inflict. If the charismatic faith 'healer' lays claim to such power, under the reasons described above, it is quite likely the faith healer has broken the commandment of bearing false testimony (Exodus 20:16). Quite simply, a faith 'healer' is not telling the truth about the claims being made.

On the topic of human health in the context of universal constancy, assuming that a universal constant would have the same properties and character the universe over, this calls into question what human existence really means in property and principle in the context of an all-loving God.

Why is the human body and physical life finite and fleeting, yet the human mind can contemplate and hypothesize about the nature of an unlimited universe? Whereas universal elements of constancy that could be considered as old as the universe itself will likely continue to exist long after human physical existence comes to its conclusion? Yet, at the same time, universal physical elements as constants, such as rocks, metals, properties of light and sound for example additionally are not known to be consciously aware of themselves or each other. Nor can they be thought to be able to contemplate or hypothesize about the unlimited nature of their existence and of the universe itself. Pointing out this contrast highlights the difference between existing and being alive.

Animals, people, and plants are physically finite. Their physical lifespan therefore is measurable by time. Yet, it seems as though universal constants cannot measure time in having (at least theoretically) infinite physical existence (matter cannot be created or destroyed). With a (theoretically) unlimited abundance of time to physically exist (in one form or another), perhaps universal constants hold time itself inside of them, rather than time being an external point of reference for them.

'Existence' and 'being' then can be thought of as two different things. This distinction helps to draw out more nuanced meaning in phrases such as 'human life', 'human being', and 'human existence'. Taking 'being' and 'existence' for a point further differentiation, 'human being' pertains more to a *part* of existence. A rock could not really be called 'rock being' in the same way, yet it can be a rock in its existence. Even when examining states of matter, say in the sense of rock as lava, those are not really the same states of 'being' in the same quality as in 'being human.' In the absence of conscious awareness, infinite matter has no knowledge of the value of its properties. Perhaps universal constants function in the human mind as externally referential validation and substantiation of the human concept of the fleeting passage of human physical life. Given that humans can assess and measure passage of time by comparing passing moments to universal constants, this way, the idea of universal constants actually can help to provide stability and order in the human mind. Replication of logical proofs through formal logical processes is helpful to verify certainty for the human mind, especially when replication of a logical procedure is completed by independent and disco-ordinated sources because repeatable results help to create intersubjective certainty. In ability to test for constancy and for test results to be replicable, the scientific method and formal methods of logical understanding help to substantiate and verify the idea that something is 'true' and perhaps even 'real' in the physical world (physics) sense of the word and helps to draw out more nuanced meaning in phrases such as 'human life', 'human being', and 'human existence'.

Whether the universe is thought to be boundless, infinite, or even if it is thought to have boundaries or to be finite itself, to group math, science, physics, chemistry, or any area of study that involves scientific method, or the process of formal logic into a single category, will be deployed in this section for the purposes of thought experimentation.

It is hoped this will help demonstrate what is meant by the title of this chapter. For the proposal that logic is 'parametric' and therefore limited, Gödel's Incompleteness Theorems will show their strength in demonstration how difficult the task to find completeness in the idea that something can be axiomatically true (universally constant and consistent). To find a non-self-referential concept containing no internal contradiction, no incompleteness, and no inconsistency, or to find a completely consistent set of truths or single truth that requires no external validation, or point of reference, is an extraordinary quest for meaning, and underlays the reason people find fulfillment in seeking out greater meaning in acknowledgment of human limitations.

That a set of symbols might contain meaning will be irrelevant for the experiment in logic at this time, rather, the use of ordered sets of symbols irrespective of their meaning (symbols are being considered here to hold representational properties of axiom, given that symbols are thought of typically to represent and hold meaning within them) are going to be deployed to demonstrate the difficulty found in searching for universal certainty as Gödel's theorems can be used to call into question. For the experiment below, ordinal numbers will be the kind of symbols used in the thought experiment.

Every Time a Logical Parameter is Successfully Breached through Scientific Discovery, New Parameters are Revealed

In a class of twenty-five 2nd grade students hungry for understanding and wisdom, a question might be posed: Does 4+5=9? The students might be offered the opportunity to resolve the quest for knowledge in a completely open-ended way. Meaning students can try to resolve the question of how 9 is formed by any way they choose.

- Perhaps some of the students form a team to collaborate and to tackle the problem head-on using combined brainpower.
- Perhaps others pair up to devise a system or method that consistently and repeatedly works to find the 'answer'.
- Still, other enterprising students might search the classroom for physical objects and count them to find out if saying that 4+5 is the same somehow as saying '9', and conversely that the symbol '9' is an accurate characterization of the properties of '4' and '5' objects combined.

The 3rd group of students listed above might find a package of crayons and count out 4, count out 5 more, and then line up crayon after crayon in the set of 4 crayons, then in the set of 5 crayons, then lineup both sets alongside each other, and agree they have all witnessed (have had intersubjective experience) or become aware that a newly emerged set: '9' has come into existence.

The students in this group all testify to the extended length of 9 crayons when they recall and mentally compare the length of the previously existing set of 4 and the previously existing set of 5 independently drawn out from each of their minds. After having witnessed and testified to the emergence of such properties of the newly created set as described above, with all 9 crayons in both ordered sets lined together and ordered in a lengthened row, this group, as a final task, count the crayons one by one in the created sum total of the two previous sets of 4 and 5 crayons now newly merged into a single set to determine if it can be said that it is true that what was 4 and 5 separately are now 9 together. In the context of putting a set of 4 crayons together with a set 5 crayons, and by declaring them bound into a new set with a new property, they conclude that by way of their methodology (in the 2nd grade sense), that yes, they are reasonably confident that a set of 4 crayons and a set of 5 combined together and then counted one after the other, has established a new, lengthier set of crayons that can be called 9 (crayons).

Toward the end of the open-ended quest for truth, and more importantly for the students, toward the beginning of lunch, the ambitious class begins to self-organize by congregating to compare and share their results. If the conclusions are thought to be unconvincing, or yet undetermined, perhaps the class peppers each other with questions and clarification about their findings. Perhaps they will compare methodologies used by every group, pair, or individual to come to their conclusions about the nature of 9, such that 7-year-olds might do in their 7-year-old way. Inside the parameters of 4 walls, a ceiling, and the floor of the classroom, a self-contained, independent and experimental mathematics laboratory has emerged in which discoveries about something of the truth about 9 took place. Within the boundaries of the classroom space, just like in any classroom with walls and a roof and a floor underneath, and under the parameters of the instructions given by the teacher for the challenge of the math quest itself, did this class of 2nd grade scholars find out the truth about 9? Do 4 and 5 when somehow put together in a particular way organize to become 9? If the entire class of twenty-five students came to the same conclusion, that yes, 9 is the same as 4+5, does that mean that mathematical 9 can be declaratively called a truth? If only twenty of the twenty-five students had the same outcome and concluded that yes, 4+5 is the same as 9, does their majority of twenty same answers override the five students with a different outcome give greater weight to the claim that 'truth' has been established? What if six of the twenty students who agreed with and supported the claim that 9 was as it was thought to be, had simply made random guesses, or went along with their friends' ideas to gain favor with them, without any effort or explanation put into their witness and testimony to the claim of the truth about 9? If the class was split evenly in their findings, or if twenty of the students found 4+5 to be 11, yet could reasonably explain their processes, used several uncoordinated processes, and only the remaining five students found 4+5 to result in 9, how would this confuse the situation?

If the 2nd grade classroom across the hall carried out the same quest to seek out the truth about 9 in their own self-contained and independent experimental mathematics laboratory, what were their findings? Would it matter if the 1st graders (or even the 4th graders) attained a consistent and agreed upon finding among themselves, but they found on the balance of results that 4+5=7? Suppose that another 4th grade class conducted the quest as well and concluded that not only is 4+5 the same as 9, but at the same time 2+7 is the same as 9, what would be the implications for certainty in the 2nd grade class regarding the true nature of

9? Are 2+7 and 4+5 consistent, or do they call into question the absolute terms of the constant properties of 9, and the composition of 9 as containing internal coherence and free from internal contradiction? For the assurance of understood certainty for the originally mentioned 2nd grade class, what are the implications of these independent findings and differences in formal processes of study? If 2+7 and 4+5 are somehow 9 independently by expression, in outcome, in meaning, in properties or principles contained within, even within object physical properties, then, is that to say that 9 can differ depending on context? Perhaps 9 as an entity in the 5th grade room found that 3+6 is the same as 9, and still, another student working on the question of the truth about 9 in the 3rd grade classroom noticed when looking across the front of the desk of another student that the image of 9 as seen from the opposite direction shared similar visual properties with 6!

When or where then can 9 be declared to hold constancy? If at all? If the classroom down the hall had no knowledge of the findings of the classroom at the other end of the hall, and accepted 9 for what they concluded it to be, and with differing results and experiences with 9 as were treated conclusive in another classroom, in absolute terms then, has understanding about 9 really complete in either room? or any room? Or in any classroom in another school, or in any part of the city? In the country? And then of course, by extension, is there absolute understanding in outwardly expanded parameters ad infinitum, really in any place? How can there really be certainty other than through agreements? Are the theorems developed about 9 in each class incomplete in their absence of universal or at least, in the absence of further experimentation with properties of 9? With the number 9 and its properties put to rest for the moment, what conclusions, if any, can be drawn from such an all at once robust, engrossing, boring, lively, dulling, meaningless, thought-provoking, futile, meaningful, and perhaps at least at minimum healthy exploration and quest for truth amongst 2nd graders?

Many things immediately become apparent in the use of the process of scientific inquiry for exploration and discovery, and formal procedures in understanding 9. It is apparent that scientific process and inquiry finds ways to explain, to learn about, to decide upon, to describe, or to understand something of the properties of what makes object 9, 9. It is even possible to use scientific process and inquiry to further devise abstract schematic properties and/or principles of 9 that might apply directly to 9, or that might apply to 9 that will be of benefit for greater understanding of less tangible aspects of the created world.

It is reasonable to suggest that logic as a scientific process of inquiry used to examine and understand physical properties and principles of physical properties of the world, are based upon defining parametrical boundaries (sets) by its very nature to be able to make distinctions between and among objects, and to create a sense of orderliness within the human mind. Efforts to try to explain, to classify, or to organize various properties and characteristics of things and by extension, to do the same even with ideas, whether physical objects from the natural world like rocks, human-made products and inventions like candy or cars, or collections of symbols such as numbers, similar color qualities, by naming planets and categorizing their attributes in the solar system, the measurement of the passage of time, portioning out quantities of liquids, the organization of sound into sets (like notes in a C major scale), or the development and ordering of the periodic table of elements; all of these systems of organization help humanity to create (or identify) a sense of orderliness in what would otherwise present to the human mind as a chaotic and unpredictable universe (whether the universe contains some kind of pre-designed ordered or not).

Logical systems are thus based upon greater and greater or smaller and smaller boundaries of distinction and difference (parameters). If this were not done, or, if humans were not capable of constructing (or identifying) such a way of understanding and relating the properties of like objects and dissimilar objects to each and from each other, human civilization could not be as it is today. *As an unlimited creative tool, parametric logic opens many possibilities to generate and experiment with new ideas. While at the same time, as a tool of explanation or identification, parametric logic is one of drawing up boundaries and closing off 'externalities' and 'irrelevances'.*

Parametric logic is strong as a tool to organize and to classify objects and ideas into collections and sets. When logic is used in this way, parameters help to substantiate reality. By way of creating points of reference between 'this' and 'that', the toolkit of parametric logic helps to distinguish that 'this' cannot' be 'that', and as such 'this' and 'that' can be seen as distinct entities from one another (whatever 'this' and 'that' objects are being distinguished from each other and classified into categories).

With classification comes opportunity for the application and use of sets of objects (and/or ideas) to perform functions (this could include static functions such as simply grouping objects and/or ideas by comparable properties and leaving it at that). In terms of active functions applied to sets, the scientific benefit to creating and binding sets within parameters (physically and tangibly, or abstractly, or by some combination), means that variables can be inserted into the set or can be isolated from or drawn from the set, or, sets can be combined, extended, or stacked for example, to create new sets for greater purpose or greater understanding.

Applications of formal scientific and logical procedures have been of immense benefit in the fields of science, medicine, physics, and engineering resulting in material improvement and improvements to the physical health of humanity, even to the degree that like spiritual understanding has undergone in the 21st century the process of scientific process is beginning to be taken for granted where the axiom of 'trust science' or 'trust technology' is invoked (whatever these ideas mean).

In conclusion, experimentation on the limitations of logic to understand the nature of the physical universe, is to say that under Godel's Incompleteness Theorems, logic and systems of logical understanding are very much unstable in the sense that scientific validity is based on agreements to substantiate what is plausible and certain. Also, scientific and logical methods of understanding are more effective with the tangible and object part of reality, but fair worse in answering questions of abstraction and intangibility of experience (qualia). Therefore, scientific methods do not provide a guarantee of absolute universal certainty because it is impossible to know how aspects of object reality will function across all situations or in all parts of the universe yet unexplored. Further to this, as seen in microcosm with the elementary school thought experiment using the number 9, people often agree that an intersubjective experience occurred, but still, the details of intersubjective experience might be disagreed upon. This was seen in the search for an absolute guarantee of universal constancy in mathematics, and this way of seeing limits of logical understanding can be extended out to other areas of rational scientific inquiry.

That logic is used to create finite restrictions to understand, suggests that logical systems can be surpassed where leaps are made in thinking in the absence of complete knowledge. David Hume (1711-1776) proposed that to get at the moral aspects of right and wrong in human understanding, a 'leap' has to be made to the experience of felt injustice (Law,

2007, pp. 290-291). Intangible aspects of morality cannot be reached through by logical conclusions alone according to Hume, nor do people necessarily have agreed upon intersubjective experience of what is right or wrong in the experience of felt injustice, although many, if not most people have a sense of what is just through this kind of felt experience (Law, 2007, pp. 290-291). 20th century French Philosopher and Poet Gaston Bachelard (1884-1962) came to much the same conclusion, referring to reliance by scientists on what he called 'epistemological break', where leaps to conclusions are made, or where various theories and scientific methods are applied to fields of study differently by different scientists (Gaston Bachelard Quotes - 2 Science Quotes - Dictionary of Science Quotations and Scientist Quotes).

The idea of absolute universal Truth is elusive in the immensity of universal proportions. Finding something of that quality by rational means is so very elusive that it can hopefully be seen that logic is useful, but limited as a tool of understanding, and that is a plausible and even valid conclusion to draw, necessitating spiritual development where reason alone cannot fully offer comfort for life's trials and hardships. However, if a person seeks spiritual understanding in some way, to abandon scientific inquiry or to abandon logical processes of thought, or logic itself would of course be sheer madness for any truly conscious and thinking person. Spiritual pursuit rightly ought to be backstopped with complementary understanding found in logical and reasoned thinking, and similarly, the overly scientific and logical mind would benefit from balancing hardline rationalism with spiritual considerations.

Systems of Logic Offer Reasonable Assurance of Certainty Through Intersubjective Agreement but are Surpassed by "Epistemological Breaks"

When parametric logic is used as a tool of ordering of what is a seemingly chaotic and/or limitless universe, corresponding improvements in material prosperity, and improvements to health and well-being are possible. The idea to create (or discovering that it is possible to create) sets of objects and ideas containing certain properties or qualities that bind them together by parameters has been of tremendous benefit and service to humanity.

For people who can competently and capably make use of such tools of discovery and innovation, to express the sentiment that the study of science leads to improvements in human well-being is embarrassingly, and perhaps even underwhelmingly a tremendous understatement of the achievements made in scientific advancement during the last several centuries. This, while typing on a web-enabled computer with access to the sum total of uploaded human knowledge just a few clicks away. Yet, in the application of Godel's Theorems to the realm of mathematics and its logic, as relatable to hard sciences, demonstration of limits in hard science in their characteristic and dispassionate 'make of it what you will' mindset cannot really explain or offer anything of a universal 'why' or provide anything more of 'meaning' in the parametrically bound way of discovering 'causal' or 'correlative' 'whys'. For this reason, scientific logic cannot really be a source of intangible theological or philosophical assurances of universal constancy or certainty because the premise of logical formalism is one of objective understanding at its outset. Yet, at the same time, logical formalism used in science can push back firmly, and with quite great resistance to Gödel's Incompleteness Theorems.

Please see **Plato: The Republic Book VI, 'The Allegory of the Cave'** (ca. 380-350 BCE) for further understanding Parametric Logic.

Please see **Aristotle: Physics** (ca. 350 BCE) for further understanding of the foundations of scientific logic.

For relevant New Testament scripture please see: **Matthew 7:24, Romans 12:2, James 3: 13-18, and Ephesians 5: 15-17**

Please see the **Old Testament: Book of Proverbs** additionally as the 'go-to' Biblical source for contemplation of logical principles of wisdom written in axiomatic language.

Experimentation with Limits of Moral Logic

The final experimentation with the limits of logic in this volume will be centered on moral reasoning and its relationship to axiomatic logic and formal logical procedures in the Roman and Greek Classical Tradition.

Once again, Kurt Gödel's Incompleteness Theorems will be used as a tool of assessment and analysis to examine potential internal inconsistency, breakdowns in logical coherence, and self-referential validation that might be contained within a small sampling of the body of Greek classical scholarship pertaining to intellectual understanding of morality and ethics. The tradition of classical scholarship is a body of work of such high quality that it is perhaps a formidable opponent to Gödel's Incompleteness Theorems and more-so to the minimal capacities of the author to engage with classical scholarship this way. However, this experimentation will be carried out anyway, in the interest of perhaps at be least minimal furtherance of understanding of what constitutes universal principles of moral truth.

Jesus was able to overturn previously held conceptions about morality and God, against the backdrop of intellectual a high and rigorous standard of existing moral scholarship available in the Roman Empire during the turn from B.C.E to C.E. The deployment of the Incompleteness Theorems in this section will aid in the assessment of the benefits and drawbacks in developing moral character and personal standards of ethical living by way of various intellectual logical frameworks. For points of contrast, the benefits of developing moral character and ethical standards of living when led by the heart and the case for accepting the message of Jesus by freedom of conscience has already been firmly established in Chapter Two and presents a stronger case on its own for morality of the heart than Gödel's Theorems can really offer. The author acknowledges strengths and some commonalities that may be found among various religious/spiritual approaches to moral and ethical standards of custom, belief, and practice. This section will examine the development of the Greek intellectual tradition of moral and ethical standards and will apply the lens of Gödel's Incompleteness Theorems to several examples of Ancient Greek scholarship.

Because the Greek, and its outgrowth, the Roman tradition of moral and ethical scholarship, was highly focused on developing an understanding of the nature of morality and ethical life in an intellectual way, and because it would have thus been very much the predominant way of understanding morality during Jesus' life, the focus on the early Greek body of logic pertaining to morality and ethics will likely be found to contain proposed systems of moral consistency, but might perhaps be limited in ability to be externally verifiable. By keeping this in mind, it will be shown that well-reasoned arguments in Ancient Greek philosophy encouraged further systems of reasoning and argumentation, but did not cross the threshold to accept limits of knowledge, nor did they lead to the pursuit of faith or even a Hume or Bachelard type leap in moral cognition where gaps in incomplete logic systems could not be proven to be completely consistent.

In this sense, the foundational figures of classical moral logic offer the 'how' of ethical living and reasons for the 'how', but leave undecidability in the 'why' of life, and in limited knowledge, propose, but do not offer assurance of life beyond death. A brief but formidable undertaking will be attempted in this section. In a limited sampling of resources from the development of classical understanding of logic as it pertains to morality and ethical living, this section is not intended to minimize the impact the foundational figures Western thought have had, nor is it to generalize out to a complete understanding of the early tradition where in the lengthy span of time of the Greek and Roman civilizations, many people wrote differing and diverse viewpoints and developed a range of theories on the subjects of morality, ethics, and the good life during that time.

By limiting this experiment to three early philosophers and works roughly corresponding to the time of the intertestamentary period, and seeing how they came to investigate and explain questions of universal morality, it is hoped that in microcosm, it will be shown even in the efforts of Plato and Aristotle, and in Plato's characterization of the beliefs Socrates, what views they would have held regarding questions of life, morality, death and God, that there is agreement in the finality of physical death, and if two of three of them believed there is life beyond death, then to earn a good eternal existence, they speculated it must be earned through deeds of ethical living, as in works-based, which as a concept, Jesus taught to be false (as in the Parable of the Vineyard Workers, see Chapter Four), and as Paul successfully argued against in Epistle to the Romans (see Chapter Two).

In *The Last Days of Socrates* from his work: *Phaedo* (ca. 360 B.C.E), Plato created a dialogue in which he has Socrates outline his beliefs on life, death, morality, ethics, and the God, and the afterlife upon physical death. The dialogue is in Socratic format of questions and responses, and is set against the backdrop of Socrates being sentenced to death.

During the dialogue, Socrates discusses whether the human soul as the capacity for immortality, and when physical death occurs, the soul becomes separated from the human body, that in preparation of the soul for its departure to into the spiritual realm, the emphasis of the physical person must revolve around making good decisions and positive interactions and deeds with other people. To accomplish these, Plato has Socrates describe living a good life to be one of living by 'virtue' and a moral 'rightness' that is in keeping with the nature of divine order and the properties of goodness that are universal.

Plato did not characterize Socrates as believing in a single God as a monotheistic entity. However, in Plato's characterization, Plato did suggest that Socrates' might have tilted toward the belief in something of a single source of supernatural 'Good'. In his sentence to death, Plato contends that Socrates was charged with questioning beliefs about the existence of a multitude of deities, although Socrates was not in disagreement that such things might exist. That Plato characterized Socrates as believing in living a life of virtue would more greatly align one's soul with divine supernatural order, Plato in his own work took Socrates' reasoning on this and matters of good deed further.

In Plato's: *The Republic* (ca. 375 B.C.E.) he firms up the idea of universal order and supernatural good into an idea of a single supernatural entity of good form that is perfect and contains the properties of all morality. A person must strive to live a life of absolute goodness as best as possible, for their soul to become in-line and itself ordered with this singular and perfect form of the supernatural. In Plato's line of reasoning, there is something beyond physical death, and he proposes that the human soul would experience it upon its separation, and in its departure and travel into the afterlife. This shaped his belief on what a universal system of morality might entail. For Plato, acts of good deed while physically alive would be helpful for the soul to experience something of eternal goodness in its time after separation from its physical body.

In Aristotle's philosophy of morality and ethical living, as characterized in: *Nichomachean Ethics* (ca. 350 B.C.E.), Aristotle reasoned that the highest standard of human morality is intellectually premised on virtue, and the character trait of virtue as it pertains to the interactions among people. Aristotle divides the concept of virtue into various sub-attributes. However, in Aristotle's viewpoint, life does not continue in any way beyond physical death. As such, a person can make the most of this life by being of good character and being known to be remembered as virtuous for fulfillment.

While the Incompleteness Theorems could be seen as strongly pushed back against by the early Greek Philosophers in the search for absolute universal truth, singularity of the divine, or systems of universal truth. When testing the limits of logic in classical Greek foundational thought, the Greek philosophers were masters of thinking through systems of logic, and were skilled in their ability to reason through difficult questions and ideas. Yet, in a more broadly defined way, Gödel has already demonstrated the limitations of their work. Not in the sense of axioms as a form of absolute truth, and not so in the systems of logical procedure themselves through which the Greek philosophers came to their conclusions. However, perhaps in limited prior precedents for comparative points of reference, the Greek philosophers were competently developing the beginnings of an understanding of the supernatural world from the ground up. Yet, in this, perhaps they could not really make a leap to faith in self-awareness of their own limits of reasoning or incompleteness of knowing.

In the development and expression of skillful, yet still, closed loop logical argumentation, the early philosophers achieved a high standard of intellectual rigor, with much logical consistency as was their craft. In Plato's *Allegory of the Cave*, from *The Republic*, he might have achieved something of the understanding of the limits of logic as being parametric in the absence of external reference, yet in the three works of the philosophers a described above, their logical systems are perhaps consistent and contain an element approaching completeness in form, but remain self-referential in the absence of limited prior precedent of comparative attainment of understanding in the classical Greek scholarly tradition. What is unknown of course is the discourse and informal conversations Socrates, Plato, and Aristotle would have engaged in with their colleagues and each other at the time, and how it would have influenced their thinking and writing.

For further exploration of the topic of Morality and Ethics in Classical Greece please see:

Plato: ***Phaedo* (The Last Days of Socrates)** (ca. 360 B.C.E)

Plato: ***The Republic*** (ca. 375 B.C.E.)

Aristotle: ***Nichomachean Ethics*** (ca. 350 B.CE.)

Chapter 6

Anticipated Criticisms Arising and Defense of Ideas Presented

"Who is the great dragon whom the spirit will no longer call lord and god? "Thou shalt" is the name of the great dragon. But the spirit of the lion says, "I will." "Thou shalt" lies in his way, sparkling like gold, an animal covered with scales; and on every scale shines a golden "thou shalt." Values, thousands of years old, shine on these scales; and thus speaks the mightiest of all the dragons: "All value of all things shines on me. All value has long been created, and I am all created value. Verily, there shall be no more 'I will.' "Thus speaks the dragon."

(Thus Spoke Zarathustra, Frederich Nietzsche) (1885)

Defense from External Philosophical and Scientific Criticism: The Quest for Meaning is Universal Across Fields of Study

Despite the title of this book, hopefully it has been demonstrated that it is not one of existential absurdism, nor existential nihilism, nor any philosophical nor political 'ism' at all. However, during writing, identification of similarities with some of these philosophies has surfaced. The idea that logic, while a useful tool, is not necessarily a source of spiritual fulfillment, is not to imply that with humanity's overestimation of logical capabilities, is the same as saying that life is in any way meaningless or absurd. Logical formalism, rational philosophy, scientific methods, study of historical precedents, the social scientists' methodology for studying human nature and affairs, are all important ways to learn from and to improve the human condition. They are of course drawn from human cognitive capacities and exercised by building meaning from information and observations that the cognitive mind draws from the external world. That humanity overestimates collective understanding of the nature of the cosmos, or is limited in understanding what awaits upon physical death, and that people do not fully understand the nature of God, is not to say that the uses of formal logic should be excluded as a tool of free inquiry to at least continue to try. To give up and declare or admit defeat in the pursuit of such understanding, would be to give up on part of innate human nature to seek higher purpose through the use of reason in the attainment of knowledge. It has hopefully been recognized through this writing that faith in God helps to steady the course of intellectual uncertainty and doubt and this can be balanced by not discrediting spiritual pursuit toward the same understanding, and by not immediately dismissing spiritual understanding as an invalid way of making sense of the universe.

Without having drawn intentionally from eastern spiritual philosophy, in undertaking paradoxical problems as a source of Christian spiritual knowledge, there are some parallels that might be pointed out between the ways proposed in this volume to approaching contradictions contained within Christian scripture, and in the way that Buddhist philosophy is practiced and undertaken. The compossible ~ incompossible construct was deployed as a tool for examining contradictions including contradiction within oneself, within matters of worldly concern, and within matters of scriptural and spiritual thought. By applying rationalism toward understanding biblical paradoxes, and by applying the paradox of undecidability to formal logic to make an improved case for spiritual understanding, commonalities with Buddhist practices of contemplating contradiction became apparent. To explore Christianity in this way has parallels with the way students of Buddhism are given Koans by their teacher upon which to meditate. Koans are a riddle or paradox upon which the

Buddhist student is to meditate. However, the students are not meditating upon the Koan to find the answer to the riddle or paradox, but rather, they meditate upon contradiction to open their minds to greater consciousness (Reese, 1999, p. 382). Typically, in the Western philosophical tradition of reasoning and formal logic, identification of paradox discredits an internally contradictory statement as fallacy and therefore such a statement becomes deemed to be 'invalid'. Yet, there may be benefit to the Christian philosophical tradition to draw from the Buddhist approach to understanding theological confounds in the Bible this way. As seen, the Christian Bible is not without seeming contradiction. Established contradictions in Christian theology for example include:

1) The concept of the unlimited goodness of God versus the problem of evil and suffering

2) The paradox of free will versus determinism

3) God as the Holy Trinity versus Christianity as a monotheistic tradition

Indeed, these are broader and well-known criticisms of the Christian tradition, and similar examples of contradiction in scripture can be found and teased apart as well. However the point here is to propose that like the Buddhist meditative reflection on Koans, Christians would benefit from the meditative practice of prayer as a channel to finding peace in the limitations of logical understanding of God. While the benefits of prayer as a Church community is an established practice, as well as individual prayer, for valid reasons, Christians pray directly 'for' things. This could include, for example, the well-being of others who are perhaps ill, for one's own well-being, or for peace in a particular situation of personal, or societal strife.

Again, these are significant for individual Christians and as a Christian community. Yet, overemphasis on praying 'for' may result in neglecting the practice as described above in praying 'upon' questions of an existential nature. Christians tend to pray 'for' the welfare of humanity directly. Yet, perhaps by praying more broadly 'upon' deeper questions of the Christian faith tradition and its seeming problems of contradiction, it could be helpful for fulfilling the improvement to humanity by seeking greater scriptural clarity this way as well. All of this can occur in addition to carrying out the work of improvement to the human condition through continued growth and advancement in areas of philosophical and scientific understanding. Acknowledging the benefits of a broad range of approaches to human understanding is to say that rationalism and spirituality are not incompatible, nor are they at all incompossible as an inherent contradiction. Christian theology might benefit from adopting the move in rationalist philosophy away from regarding 'paradox' as a mystical concept. Instead, perhaps by viewing paradoxes as theorems yet proven or unproven would be beneficial. Alternatively, including study of scriptural paradox as a form of mysticism, under the framework of free inquiry, why not pursue both ways of understanding, and seek common ground between them?

Defense from External Religious Criticism: Ritualism is not Analogous to Expressive and Meaningful Worship

Like carrying out a formal logic process, ritualism contains many similarities. Like religious ritualism, formal logic process can be easily replicated and is rightfully applied to the work of history, philosophy, scientific research or study and even to spiritual studies. No doubt, the idea that a procedure can be independently replicated and verified helps to create certainty and implies that something in the physical world is 'valid'. The benefits being seen in the material abundance of the west such as scientific advancements, improvements in medicine, new inventions, and any number of feats of improvement and understanding where people have succeeded greatly.

Both the strength and limitation of such ways of understanding is in the parametric nature of isolating variability under certain conditions. For example, a self-contained logical statement can be valid despite its initial premise being false. A self-contained logical statement can be true despite being in error externally. To create a parameter, and then to insert and experiment with variability within the parameter, means that the variables can be manipulated within the set to create a sense of order. Yet, despite doing so, if the premise at the start is false, the procedures performed inside the parameter may seem valid in themselves, with no inherent contradiction, yet, they may be lacking in external validity or purpose, even if it can be replicated independently.

If this kind of fallacy is applied to religious behavior, the shortcoming of formal religious ritualism can be seen. This is where the premise of such behavior requires scrutiny. Does ritualized repetition will truth into existence? Does tradition imply certainty? If things are done simply because 'that's the way they have always been done', does that imply validity? Of course, tradition has symbolism built into it. Tradition creates meaning in the sense of identifiable origins of the tradition and ties to ancestral and cultural heritage for example. Yet, if the premise of the ritual is faulty, if the individual must surrender to the collective (or is forced to), if the premise is to exclude others, or to grant the perception of favor to people who are amenable to comply with the ritual for its own sake, then there lies the problem with the focus on ritualism in religion, whether within a Christian organization or in a non-Christian religious organization.

Who benefits? Is there fear of reprisal induced into adherents, or is there othering of the non-compliant? In the absence of external and independent reference checks or points, or in the absence of a point of comparison or contrast, people who live in such a limited way have become part of the 'set' in the parameters of a self-contained logic system. If the operations performed and contained within the ritualistic parameter have applications elsewhere, would it not be best to put them to the marketplace of spiritual ideas? Similarly, if the self-contained logic of the religious practice is discouraged from being challenged, then does faith in the religious practice and its claimed benefit really exist? Sameness is not synonymous with truth. To seek to create truth from a faulty premise and to replicate the process will not will truth into existence through the repetition. How often in church is the refrain heard: 'but that's the way we've always done it!' The times in which one lives may call for a fresh approach to the 'old story'. However, if the 'old story' is of a solid premise and foundation, it will support and be able to withstand a shift in what might seem like parametric logic.

The purpose of a church service ought not to be for its own sake. A church service might contain formal order and tradition. It might contain meaningful practices and customs such as communion, song, testimony, scripture lessons, and prayer for example. However, these things are not for their own sake, but more-so to move or to inspire the attendee to act. Sunday is seen as the beginning of the week for this reason. By spiritually preparing for what difficulties and challenges the week ahead might contain, the Christian will begin on solid footing.

If the premise of Christianity is built on the greatest of the commandments as Jesus taught, that kind of firm foundation justifies the expression of worship irrespective of the parameters of the church building and the format of worship. Invitation to free participation to one's personal comfort-level rather than focusing on rigid adherence to rules for their own sake means individuals do not lose themselves in a collective mindset.

While rigid ritualism creates order, but, if it requires strict enforcement to be upheld, or if it requires protection from external influence to retain its 'validity', perhaps it needs to be asked why? A closed set is confined by its own parameters, yet inevitably, undecidable influence will become infused into the self-affirming closed loop parameters. Benefits of formal doctrine might perhaps surface minimally here, despite previous criticism within this book. This is to propose that optimal use of doctrine or codification of religious or spiritual principles for a religious organization ought to be stripped down and limited only to what is essential to fulfill scripture. Anything beyond that essential purpose can be seen as frivolous, even harmful especially if a spiritual organization's doctrine is excessive, or overemphasized. Excessive requirement to adhere to customary habit and cultural practice for their own sake means that tribalism and politicization risk becoming infused into the articles of spiritual faith, and the codification of doctrine enters the realm of dogma and indoctrination and all the problems resulting from them.

Defense from Internal Christian Criticism: "Follow me, and I will make you fishers of men!" (Matthew 4:19)

What does it mean when someone says they are 'God fearing' or if someone makes such a statement as 'he put the fear of God into him' for example? Is that really in the overarching spirit of the Gospel message?

Certainly, there are many Christian traditions that claim (and perhaps with a degree of merit) that being 'God fearing' is something of a virtue, or to 'have the fear of God' put into someone, might be viewed as a way of helping to ensure that poor conduct is not repeated. Indeed, there is some value in having a sense of fear of consequence for behavior when behavior leans toward being harmful for oneself or others. Yet, is that the message of Jesus? Is 'fear God or else' a sustainable spiritual mindset? Does fear lead to deepening understanding of faith or growth in spiritual maturity? If a person is conditioned to act according to external approval or disapproval, will they be capable of understanding the why?

Certainly, an all-powerful God is without limited ability; warranting a reasonable and healthy degree of fear of what cannot be known by the human mind. More practically, to have the love of God 'inscribed on one's heart' as Paul describes might need to be backstopped when a person's actions maintain a pattern contrary to the good. However, the New Testament might suggest that it is not the fear of God where people should direct their spiritual mindset, but rather toward fear of one's individual capacity toward the influence of wrongdoing. That Christianity itself has been criticized for having had a negative impact throughout history is of concern in this way. Were various 'in the name of' Crusades during the Middle Ages acts of Christian aggression or tribalism? Were the cults of Waco or Jonesville built on a solid foundation of the love of Christ? What about the charismatic leadership of various megachurch organizations, or what about organizations that offer the snake-oil of false hope that literal and direct hands-on faith-healing is a credible substitute for modern scientific medicine?

Some of these message distortions again involve a closed set of parameters and offer adherents only limited and internalized beliefs, resulting from an absence of external validation. Again, the marketplace of spiritual ideas provides a check and balance against closed sets of belief. Again, if an adherent to such a system of belief is discouraged from seeking meaningful spiritual fulfillment elsewhere, it needs to be asked: why? As an egregious example, the approving religious authorities once required that a new work of Catholic writing must be stamped 'Nihil Obstat' to be permitted to be published. Nihil Obstat translates roughly to 'without objection' and it was a requirement for writing to be printed and to be declared in-line with Roman Catholic teachings. Further, as late as 1966, the Index Librorum Prohibitorum was a publicized list of books and literature banned by the Roman Catholic Church and denounced as heresy.

If the Christian message is thought to be so very easily threatened from external literature and influence this way, what does that say about the confidence the leadership of religious organizations have in their belief about their own message? What does that say about how much confidence leadership has in their adherents' spiritual wherewithal and maturity if they are 'forbidden' from engaging with 'threatening' ideas or even experiences? The *Parable of the Prodigal Son* (Luke 15: 11-32) is worth examining in this context.

Questioning restrictive organizational practices can be applicable within any Christian faith group, and as well to faith groups outside of Christianity whose messaging is thought by its leadership and adherents to be under 'threat' from external influence. It ought to be pointed out similarly, that people who 'trust the science' are restricting themselves to a limited range of ideas and scholarship when feeling somehow 'threatened' by what religious and spiritual literature might contain within it. Ideological 'threats' to people practicing a closed system of belief is the ever-present fear of external 'harmful' influence, and the possibility of internal 'mutiny' emerging from within the organization of the closed system of belief. This of course once again calls into question the genuine trust or faith held in such a 'faith- based' belief system. The tendency among the most zealous of believers in such a system will be to become more deeply and firmly restrictive in such circumstances. Yet, if the belief system is premised well, perhaps offering and advocating for genuine and free investigation into perceived ideological 'threats' would strengthen the case for the belief system itself. External checks of validation as a tool of logical discernment between systems of belief are foundational tools of understanding within human nature. Love of God and love for humanity offers defense against vicious ideologies that intentionally seek to influence people to be swayed from their well-premised individual agency and autonomy.

Chapter 7

Break Free from Religious Axiom and Ritualism to Experience Spiritual Fulfillment

The Apostle Paul on Spiritual Growth:

"When I was a child, I spoke and thought and reasoned as a child. But when I grew up, I put away childish things. Now we see things imperfectly as in a clouded mirror, but then we will see everything with perfect clarity. All that I know is partial and incomplete, but then I will know everything completely, just as God now knows me completely. Three things will last forever -faith, hope, and love -and the greatest of these is love."

(Romans 13: 11-13, NLT)

The message of this volume is not to say that to live by the letter of God's law and not the spirit of God's law is necessarily a problem. Nor is it to say that to coexist on this earth that people are not in need of law, spiritual or man-made, to govern human affairs and interaction. One of the conclusions drawn from undertaking this book is to say that what happens between law to law of God, under the law of God, and how the law of God is upheld is what is truly important during every person's time on earth, and in our interactions with each other. The two greatest commandments as taught by Jesus (Matthew 22:36-40) provide the framework for moral living, and can be thought of as the overall framework for the Ten Commandments delivered to Moses from God as chronicled in the Old Testament (Exodus 20). Loving God and then loving your neighbor simply put would go a long way to ease much of humanity's quarreling ways. To take this line of reasoning a step further, Jesus' Sermon on the Mount (Matthew 5:1-48) teaches humanity to keep the commandments as revealed to Moses in the Old Testament (Exodus 20:2-48) and it can be seen, Jesus goes into great depth in this message to share the ethical standard by which to do so. Imagine if people simply followed such rules for life how few problems there would be in this world (Meredith, pp. 6-7)!

If humanity, at minimum, were to simply obey such laws it may very well result in a positive outcome. However, people have the latitude of free will, accompanied of course by temptations and ill intentions tilting toward using said free will irresponsibly. To compound the problems of humanity's free will and spiritual immaturity, according to the Old Testament, people have been granted the responsibility to govern over the things of earth, as being a function of being created in God's image and likeness (Genesis 1:26-31). Although in what proportion and rendering the image and likeness might be, it has likely been drastically overestimated. However, because we are created in God's likeness, it can be inferred that we have a degree of cognitive capacity and a degree of free will under God's law as stated above, exceeding that of the creatures we are entrusted to govern.

However, if the law of God were to be simply obeyed, but not contemplated, not discussed, not debated, nor even tested, how would people possibly be able to responsibly manage the affairs of human interaction, and of the earth? That is, to provide for the well-being of other people, and to maintain the well-being of the natural world by sensible use of the earth's resources. Additionally, with things pertaining to spirituality and human ~ divine relations, due to limited human understanding, a degree of responsible testing of limits is necessary. In human ~ divine relations, this would include relations as a function of personal and collective will. It has been demonstrated that, like Adam and Eve in Genesis 3:1-24, people seek understanding greater than obedience and submission can simply provide on their own. Under human capacity for free will, people are rebellious toward obedience and submission to God in such a sense.

In the Book of Genesis, as the story goes, humanity chose to use its free will to indeed seek wisdom and understanding beyond its own capacity to handle. The Old Testament describes the result of seeking divine wisdom is to have been left and forsaken to manage earthly and material affairs, for better or for worse (Genesis 3: 22-24). The Old Testament tells the story of how God made the road to likeness of His understanding and wisdom immensely challenging for humanity. After breaching the self-contained and 'parametric' logic of the Garden of Eden so to speak, humanity, in predisposition toward antinomianism and disdain for humility and the taming of curiosity and agency, would be required to know that the knowledge and wisdom being sought, would not come easily, but rather, it would have to come through hardship and strife.

This brings to the forefront humanity's divorce from God and the innate human desire to seek Him for a close relationship once again. Through the course of being cast out into the hostile world, humanity has had to experiment with inhospitable nature to seek something of the wisdom and understanding necessary manage the affairs of earth, and to regain some knowledge and understanding of God. Superstitious acts of sacrificial appeasement, ordering of affairs a certain way, repeated ritualized behavior, even after Moses received and delivered the Ten Commandments to the Israelites, seeking a relationship with God has been the ultimate intent and purpose for being, and not just to live by divine law for its own sake, not simply to attain a certain degree of Godlike wisdom, but foremost, to regain felt spiritual nourishment and fulfillment. Yet, it seems despite even best efforts, humanity could not, and still, largely cannot get things right! This, despite even the best efforts and intent. When Jesus came, he offered clarity. Although he himself said that his message would be misused and distorted going forward (Matthew 7:15). Nonetheless, it has hopefully been demonstrated in this writing that humanity very much has free will (but parameters under which to use it), ought to very much embrace free will enthusiastically, yet practice its usage consciously and responsibly. As well, it has hopefully been shown that the intent of the law of God is to be *'inscribed on our hearts'* and this means people do not need to live out of fear of God, but rather, to live by and through the love of God, is to live with spiritual fulfillment because the love of God is the law of God.

As it has been stated in these pages many times, religious doctrine is but the interpreted human codification of spiritual rules, and is indeed something quite different from the law of God. People must take care to be mindful, and to be consciously aware of the benefits and drawbacks of systems of religious operation and doctrine, lest the person becomes engulfed in religiosity and doctrine becomes misused for material or political gain, or becomes a form of gatekeeping. If doctrine forms a complete system, or, if it is claimed to, then if it cannot be proven valid without external reference to the Holy Bible to compare with to appraise whether it meets the standard of Christian faith and organization.

Doctrine created with portions found to be external to biblical teaching unveils the limits and problems with human codification of religious belief. Even if doctrine has been created with best intentions, drift toward religiosity is an ever-present concern within any faith group. Religious doctrine, or any system of organizational belief requiring adherents to participate in biblical non-essential practices ought to be met with skepticism. What the Bible says derived from the context of the time it was created is the Christian standard of belief. This is not necessarily reflected in supplemental or extra-biblical articles of doctrine. Nor should standards of Christian belief be held in authority solely by the person with specialized claim to knowledge who teaches from the Holy Bible. It must be asked of adherents to systems of practice containing biblical non-essentialism: if people hold themselves to, or become beholden to fanaticism through ritualized expression of religious (or political) dogma, have elements of biblical non-essentialism assisted with spiritual development, or obstructed it?

Balance between reason and faith shows strength in this way. Faith beyond human knowledge does not have to exclude intellectual engagement, nor does the use of reason necessarily have to acknowledge limitations where further possibility of understanding is sought through its use. It is hoped that by having drawn a comparison between repetitive ritualized behavior and mathematical systems of ordered sets that superstitious ritualized behavior is perhaps not really of much benefit for the spiritually seeking, particularly when compelled or insisted upon through mechanisms of fear. As well, comparisons drawn among closed loop parametric logic, functions of sets within parameters, religious ritualism in the absence as function any external point of reference, are contributing factors to problems of limitation in individual spiritual growth. Personal spiritual growth becomes hampered by reflexive religious habit, and reflexive religious habit occurs in place of the conscious practice of spiritualism. Additionally, closed-loop ritualism creates problems of mind because it is logical for the human mind to require external reference points to check for understanding.

All of this means that being able to freely engage with scripture, to thoroughly question it, and also, to be able to do the same for articles of religious doctrine (within any religion) ought to be of paramount importance for individuals seeking spiritual fulfillment. Obstruction of free will, as a function of religious or political adherents being bound by parameters of closed-loop systems of self-contained 'logic' shows its negative effects in personal spiritual growth, creating meaningful religious practices, and additionally, shows its weakness in the political sphere and its affairs, where uncritical axiomatic dogma creates unnecessary emotive tension in societies.

By testing the limits of logic, or at least by showing there are limits in scientific and/or mathematical principles and practice, is to say that the physical universe is not yet even approximating being fully or completely understood. However, that people would believe that only what can be understood by scientific methods alone is true is a problem of limited understanding also. This can be taken to show that humanity is likely much farther away proportionally than might be estimated in understanding the nature of God and reality. While scientific observation and research, through its formal processes of rational logic do meet humanity's need to describe, to design, and to create things for material improvement, and health and well-being, and while these functions of course satisfy human intellectual curiosity, such methods of human activity and knowledge will still lag in being able to answer the call to the higher purpose of 'Why?'.

As a simple example to demonstrate the limits of rationalism, the law of cause and effect proposed by Sir Isaac Newton can be used or adapted to explain, to understand and to advance many scientific principles of physics, of chemistry, of biology, or geology, and even social studies, for a small sample. Yet, when applied to the basic question of what caused the universe; the question is simply unanswerable. The idea that the 'Big Bang' was the beginning of the universe might be perhaps as far away as human telescopes can view space, yet, citing parametric logic, surely, the discovery of the cause of the 'Big Bang' as one of breaching parametric logical understanding, would likely open more parameters of logic to be learned about and to be discovered.

By inserting Gödel's paradox of undecidability into this remarkably basic example of limitation in logical knowing, it clearly demonstrates the problem with closed loop systems of scientific provability. That finite people, using physically finite brains, and using finite methods of understanding can have complete understanding through limiting themselves to only one part of the brain's abilities is a problematic overestimation of human ability and over-reliance on logic. That logical methodology alone is thought of as solely reliable to fully find principles of fixed universal truth or law perhaps is to even neglect innate intuition of leaps in logic from intuition that people can make. Tools of logic from time to time do succeed in breaching their own parameters. Yet, upon having surpassed self-defined limitations, or at least, upon having surpassed the human expectation of such success, the result is the discovery of more parameters of non-understanding. This pattern will likely continue to emerge. This occurs even when unprecedented expansion of human knowledge has been achieved.

How often then does 'trusting science' take on a form of faith itself? Is that not counter to the spirit of rational inquiry in the scientific method? How often in the media or in casual chatter is the axiom of 'trust science' thoughtlessly tossed around as a point of discussion, or how often does it lend the speaker an air of quick authority in what might be spoken of to a fearful, or uncritical audience? As a thinking Christian, to acknowledge the benefit of scientific and objective study, and yet, at the same time to embrace the very paradox of existence, in our often seemingly nonsensical world, through reflection, meditation, prayer is to perhaps attain something of both material and spiritual improvement. That there is reflexive and unthinking, uncritical, and blind acceptance of the '-isms' of this world, and carelessly simple conventional wisdom to 'trust science' as the final and complete end of all understanding has hopefully been demonstrated to be an unfulfilling pursuit to both the human spirit, conscience, and to the thinking mind.

Surely there is more than what seems possible to be tangibly understood and experienced. From the very minute vantage point of humanity, the nature of the universe, reality, and God, by recognizing and acknowledging shortcomings, and with some humility before God, unburdening of the weary load of life's problems that each person carries, or inevitably will carry at some point can be relieved by accepting that there are limits to human understanding.

The human sense of proportion of everything is miniscule and minimal to the incomprehensibly vast and unlimited abilities of God. We have not yet found a calculator, a science, a computer, or a mathematical method that can accurately tabulate and account for the sum-total of goodness in God's universe, or why and how it was created. That is not to say to stop trying, but it is at least to say that people benefit from having faith in God, and that pursuing understanding of the nature of the universe, of reality, and of God is an inherently good decision. As a sensible choice, accepting the love of God is indeed compossible with the human reason for being.

Appendix I

A Practical Proposal for the Ideologically Adrift

Toward Spiritual Fulfillment by Acting Consciously in the Best Interest of Humanity (Whether the Christian Message is Accepted or Not)

While the Bible offers any number of stories and lessons from days gone by that remain very much relevant to the present time, the context under which the stories of old take place and have been documented are due their consideration. While human nature does not really change very much, it can be observed that the times do. To discredit the stories of history in terms of religious, political, intellectual, or personal life is of course folly. As is to 'reinvent the wheel' in perpetuity, as though every 'new' idea or 'advancement' is somehow 'progress' or 'progressive' simply by virtue of it presenting as being new.

History, when forgotten, ends up manifesting by replaying its tragic story in real-time, where ideology is put over human interest and well-being. In living memory, both material and technological advancements in human understanding have been dramatic, and continue to compound at an extraordinary pace. Because of this, the need for a degree of predictability and sense of order is as necessary now as much as it ever was. In current times, finding a moment for quiet spiritual reflection may require downloading an app to schedule it in would not seem out of the ordinary!

Asking people who are skeptical or perhaps in disagreement of the benefits of seeking a spiritual inner life, the question in practical terms becomes, in the age of competing '-isms', ideologies, and political movements substituting for higher purpose, how does the practice of Christianity as a tradition, or as even a 'reimagined' experience for the current age, make itself known and maintain relevance? This, while staying true to its message. How can it be understood that Christianity offers spiritual nourishment and fulfillment to anyone who seeks it? Perhaps, at least, if people even simply become aware that spiritual fulfillment is something desirable, and is something too often missing, would the Christian message be a good place to start?

Many people are devoid of spiritual reflection in the West. In the media, in society, in schools of both higher learning and trickling down to the younger ages, this problem can be quite easily observed. For the ideologically adrift, Christianity is largely being dismissed, ignored, or at worst denigrated. Of the Christian message itself? It is often generally made light of despite advancements made in human well-being in modern nations whose origins can be traced to the Christian tradition.

Perhaps, if much of humanity has an inflated sense of being made 'in God's image', as in, if people become so self-absorbed to believe they are somehow 'God-like', then do people who have this mindset among us see that the very idea of God is unnecessary or inconvenient under conditions of material advancement? Worse, maybe there are people who believe that we will usurp the idea of God somehow with our own abilities? Again, that seems to be folly because humanity's sense of proportion is proudly and vastly inflated and distorted.

Limitless in wisdom? Limitless in power? Limitless in love? To people who simply cannot find it within themselves to seek spiritual nourishment of any sort, through the

Christian experience or otherwise, to people who believe they can find the 'why' of existence through scientific method, to people who believe they can construct a computer that will be able to add up the total of the infinite, my proposal is this: Please go ahead and try! There is nothing to lose by doing so. It will likely push the boundaries of human understanding of the infinite further! I sincerely hope it does.

However, in doing so, please remember your own 'why'. That is, doing so in the spirit of the greatest two commandments. Or, if one remains unpersuaded by the idea of God as love, please remember to at least act in the spirit of the second commandment in all your endeavors.

Appendix II

Practical Suggestions for Church Communities

Christian Spiritual Fulfillment as Conscious Practice of Free Will

None of the following suggestions are meant to be proposed as new or original in any way, nor are they to be thought to be experimental along the theme of the book series, nor are they even meant necessarily to point to a new direction for the life of local congregations. Many congregations already do such things presented below quite successfully or have other superior ways that aid in ministering the Christian message to their members and to the public quite well. However, as they relate to the premise of this book, is in that the suggestions below are meant to convey the idea that practicing Christianity is done well by being conscious and thoughtful about it.

To congregations, offering from observation that much of what happens in churches often happens out of habit under the guise of 'tradition' is meant to be a gentle point of well-intentioned critique. This, while keeping in mind a degree of sensitivity toward the sea of greying heads visible from many pulpits and choir lofts in order not to disenfranchise the already faithful. With respect to tradition, tradition indeed provides a sense of stability, predictability, and order. As a concept, the assurances provided by tradition are of merit in a fast-paced and ever-changing era.

However, despite having made reference to problems with media previously in this book, to look favorably on popular media for a moment, as a point of contrast, in the 1997 film *Deconstructing Harry*, Woody Allen is credited with both writing the script and delivering the following line: "Tradition is the illusion of permanence."

While I have not seen the movie, nor fully know the context, the line resonated with me in terms of what goes on behind Church doors on any given Sunday! As such, here are some suggestions to be made consciously aware of, humbly offered to small and mid-sized congregations and leadership in the context of this book.

For Congregations: From a Church Musician's Perspective

Depending on church governance structure, and in an era of declining membership and declining church involvement, best efforts should be in place to have a committee of members with fiduciary experience handle and report on the financial health of the church to the congregation. This should be at arm's length from church leadership. The purpose of worship and the reason various people and regular members come to church or don't come varies. Try to assist the leadership team in meeting the needs of as many people as best as possible. However, understand that there comes a point at which it is each person's own responsibility to meet their own practical needs as best they can.

Encourage openness and free and rich dialogue regarding church matters. Embrace differences of opinion, accept respectful criticism and reflect on it, offer latitude, grace, and forgiveness in misunderstandings, and encourage other members and visitors to do so as well. Remember, while people may wish to have your ear, and may present a take on some point of scripture or spiritual practice that they may insist is wholly accurate, not all opinions are of similar merit or value. However, the person expressing them may simply wish to be acknowledged by at least being heard.

For Church Leadership (Including Musicians): Awareness of Personal Leadership Styles vs. Congregational Needs

Here is a Quick Self-Reflection Guide for Leadership:

Are you a 'top down' leader and directing traffic too much or do you listen to the needs of the congregation and fellow leaders to meet them where they are? This might include fulfilling a members' need to be in some kind of leadership role themselves, informally or otherwise.

Do you facilitate connection between members? As in perhaps discreetly acting behind the scenes in such a way that folks will find a meaningful connection with someone else in the congregation with whom they might not normally have engaged?

Do you encourage (intentionally), or perhaps discourage (unintentionally) others' spiritual growth? Or do you actively help congregants and other leaders to meet own their needs in a way that is meaningful to them?

What are the strengths of your church members and how can they be of service to the community?

- Who are the teachers?
- Who are the mentors?
- Who are the evangelists?
- Who knows the congregation's story and history?
- Who is musically or dramatically inclined (yet perhaps does not feel included to share their abilities)?
- Who are the helpers that make things run behind the scenes?
- Who are the innovators that can propel the church forward?
- Who are the 'schmoozers', inside and outside of church that help to invite and to retain new members?

The Distinction Between Praying 'For' vs. Praying 'Upon'

While praying for the ill, for the shut-ins, for the concerns of the community, or for resolution to ongoing conflict in the world is of great benefit for such causes, and as well, brings the church together toward a common focus, the idea of taking time to pray 'upon' matters of concern is quite different altogether. Yet, it is often overlooked as a method of prayer in its importance.

While both kinds of prayer may not offer any tangible solution to the ills of the world necessarily, but by noting the distinction in these approaches to prayer, consciously practicing one way or the other may enable greater clarity in the spiritual mindset of people who may seek to take on the world's ills in active ways.

On the Sacraments

Gently offer support for people who are visitors to your church, and for people who are new to the Christian church altogether. If possible, have a system in place, or have volunteers at the ready who can warmly and discreetly help meet the needs of newcomers. On occasion, gently remind congregants of the significance of the sacraments. This can be helpful especially when done in an informal rather than scripted way from time to time. The shift in many denominations toward communion being offered to all, and away from it being administered conditionally through requirements such as baptism or denominational membership is a good one: it is God's table, and not that of the local church or of a particular denomination.

Gently remind the congregation from time to time that administration and partaking in the sacraments is a serious undertaking to be done in faith and not merely one of performative habit. When possible, tell of the significance of communion for example, ahead of time and informally for inexperienced visitors, in addition to the prepared script for the service.

On Trying New Ways of Doing Things

When implementing a shift in congregational practice, respect individual autonomy and the comfort level people may have with new experiences. Make best efforts to consider individual people whose life history might result in their need for, and their benefit from the comfort of predictability and order of previously established worship practices that have already been established.

An impossible suggestion, but at the same time, try to make best efforts to meet the needs of more forward-looking congregation members. Offer transparency and accountability to members with respect to the intentions of the spiritual direction of the church, and provide as much advance notification as would be of benefit.

Conscious Practices for Preparing for Worship

Strive for worship that is meaningful and affirming. Prepare for worship conscientiously. Do not compel participation. Think long term and thematically. Think of in terms of *teaching* scripture whether in pastoral or musical ministry. Consult with people who might offer insight into a special service or event. Predictability creates comfort and assurance through orderliness, yet also employing spontaneity when the moment calls for it can add an element of renewal.

For all Churchgoers

Fulfill the Christian message by offering positivity, hope, assurance, and affirmation. Make it known what a joy it is to be part of the Christian community!

Works Cited

Aristotle. (ca. 4th century B.C.E., English Edition: 2022). The Art of Rhetoric. (Unknown, Trans.) London: Arcturus Holdings Limited.

Burton, H. F. (1912). The worship of the roman emperors. The Biblical World, 40(2), 88–91. https://doi.org/10.1086/474622 (Retrieved 2025)

Chadwick, O. (1975). The Early Church. Harmondsworth, UK: Penguin Books Ltd.

Chadwick, O. (1988). The Reformation. London: Penguin Books Ltd.

Clarke, J. (2018, July 6). Enrollment Trends of Christian Colleges and Universities in the

Last 30 Years. Christian Post. Retrieved 2024, from: https://www.christianpost.com/news/enrollment-trends-of-christian-colleges-and-universities-in-last-30-years.html

Crilly, T. (2011). Mathematics (Vol. The Big Questions). (S. Blackburn, Ed.) London, UK: Quercus Publishing PLC.

Dunstan, J. L. (1961). Protestantism. New York: George Braziller, Inc.

Ferguson, Niall. (2014). The Great Degeneration. New York: Penguin Books.

Gaston Bachelard Quotes - 2 Science Quotes - Dictionary of Science Quotations and Scientist Quotes (2025) Retrieved from: https://todayinsci.com/B/Bachelard_Gaston/BachelardGaston-Quotations.htm (April 14th, 2025).

Gordon, R. J. (2016). The Rise and Fall of American Growth. New Jersey: Princeton University Press.

Green, R. W. (1959). Protestantism and Capitalism: The Weber Thesis and Its Critics. Boston: D.C. Heath and Company.

Greenspan, A., & Wooldridge, A. (2018). Capitalism in America. New York: Penguin Press.

Harrington, M. (1987). The Politics at God's Funeral. New York: Viking Penguin Inc.

Hayes, M. (2007). Googling God. Mahwah, New Jersey: Paulist Press.

Hertzberg, Arthur. (1962). Judaism. New York: George Braziller, Inc.

https://en.wikisource.org/wiki/Works_of_Martin_Luther,_with_introductions_and_notes/Volume_1/Disputation_on_Indulgences#Ninety-five_Theses. (n.d.). Retrieved 2024, from Works of Martin Luther.

https://www.loc.gov/exhibits/relgion/index.html. (2024). Retrieved from Religion and the Founding of the American Republic Home.

Jacobs, L. (1984). The book of Jewish belief. Behrman House, Inc.

Kirk, R. (1992). The Roots of American Order. Washington D.C.: Regnery Gateway.

Konig, M. Ger d. Romans. (2004). Sunbury, PA: Believers Bookshelf, Inc.

MacCulloch, D. (2009). Christianity: The First Three Thousand Years. London: Penguin Books Ltd.

Meredith, R. C. (1997, January). What Is a True Christian? What Is a True Christian?, WTC Edition 2.0. San Diego, California, United States of America: Global Church of God.

Montreal Holocaust Museum. Retrieved 2025, from https://museeholocauste.ca/en/

Nietzsche, F. (1885). Thus Spake Zarathustra. (2023, Ed., & Unknown, Trans.) London: Arcturus Publishing Limited.

Nietzsche, F. (n.d.). Thus Spake Zarathustra a Book for All and None. The Gutenberg Project. Retrieved 2024, from https://www.gutenberg.org/files/1998/1998-h1998-h.htm#link2H_4_0006

Pew Research Center. (2011). Global Christianity -A Report on the Size and Distribution of the World's Christian Population. Washington D.C.: Pew Research Center. Retrieved 2024

Pew Research Center. (2018). Religious Attitudes and Identity in Western Europe. Washington D.C.: Pew Research Center. Retrieved 2024

Pew Research Center. (2024). In U.S., 41% have become more spiritual over time; fewer, more religious. Washington D.C.: Pew Research Center. Retrieved 2024

Plato. (ca. 380-351 B.C.E. Publication Date: 2004). Republic (Copyright Elizabeth Watson Scharffenberger ed.). (B. Jowett, Trans.) New York: Barnes & Noble Books.

Reese, W. L. (1999). Dictionary of Philosophy and Religion: Eastern and Western thought. Amherst, New York: Prometheus Books.

Restak, R. M. (2012). Mind (Vol. The Big Questions). (S. Blackburn, Ed.) London: Quercus Editions Ltd.

Sanchez, L.M. (2024). The Epistemological Turn of the Twentieth Century's Legal Positivism. Netherlands Journal of Legal Philosophy, 53(1), 93-120. https://doi.org/10.5553/NJLP/.000114

Seymour, M. L. (1997). American Exceptionalism: A Double-Edged Sword. New York: W.W. Norton & Company.

Tabor, James D. (2012). Paul & Jesus: How the Apostle Transformed Christianity. New York: Simon & Schuster.

The Constitution: A Collection of Historically Important Communications of the United States of America. 1776-1963 (Unaltered Republication ed.). (2014). Ashland: Bendon.

Tocqueville, A. d. (2004). Democracy in America (Complete and Unabridged ed., Vol. 1 & 2). (H. Reeve, Trans.) New York: Bantam Dell.

Vogt, B. (2011). The Church and NE Media. Huntington, Indiana: Our Sunday Visitor Publishing Division.

Walker, W. (1970). A History of the Christian Church. New York: Charles Scribner's Sons.

Wills, G. (2008). Head and Heart: A History of Christianity in America. London: Penguin Books Ltd.

Zahavi, D. (2006 12(2), May). Two takes on a one-level account of consciousness. (Retrieved 2024) from researchgate.net: https://psyche.cs.monash.edu.au/

Further Reading

- Augustine. (1998). Confessions (M. Boulding, Trans.). Vintage Books.
- Ayer, A. J. (1988). Bertrand Russell. The University of Chicago Press.
- Berto, F. (2009). There's something about Gödel: The complete guide to the incompleteness theorem. Wiley-Blackwell.
- Blomberg, C. L. (2009). Jesus and the Gospels. B & H Publishing Group.
- Budiansky, S. (2021). Journey to the edge of reason: The life of Kurt Gödel. W.W. Norton and Company Inc.
- Dunstan, J. L. (1961). Protestantism. George Braziller, Inc.
- Durkheim, E. (1995). The elementary forms of religious life (K. E. Fields, Trans.). The Free Press.
- Gordon, R. J. (2016). The rise and fall of American growth. Princeton University Press.
- Green, R. W. (1959). Protestantism and capitalism: The Weber thesis and its critics. D.C. Heath and Company.
- Greenspan, A., & Wooldridge, A. (2018). Capitalism in America. Penguin Press.
- Harrington, M. (1987). The politics at God's funeral. Viking Penguin Inc.
- Jacobs, L. (1984). The book of Jewish belief. Behrman House, Inc.
- James, W. (2002). The varieties of religious experience. Random House Inc.
- Küng, H. (1965). The church and freedom (C. Hastings, Trans.). Sheed and Ward Ltd.

- Laurie, G. (Ed.). (2004). How to find God: New Testament, New Living Translation (2nd ed.). Tyndale House Publishers, Inc.
- Mitchell, S. (Trans.). (1992). The book of Job. Harper Perennial.
- New American Standard Bible. (1977). The Lockman Foundation.
- Nietzsche, F. (2022). Beyond good and evil. Arcturus Publishing Limited.
- Nietzsche, F. (2022). On the genealogy of morals. Arcturus Publishing Limited.
- Pew Research Center. (2011). Global Christianity: A report on the size and distribution of the world's Christian population.
- Pew Research Center. (2018). Being Christian in Western Europe.
- Pew Research Center. (2024). Around 4 in 10 Americans have become more spiritual over time; fewer have become more religious.
- Reese, W. L. (1999). Dictionary of philosophy and religion: Eastern and Western thought. Prometheus Books.
- Russell, B. (2004). Introduction to mathematical philosophy. Routledge.
- Russell, B. (2014). The art of philosophizing and other essays. Rowman & Littlefield Publishers, Inc.
- Seymour, M. L. (1997). American exceptionalism: A double-edged sword. W.W. Norton & Company.
- Smith, P. (2013). An introduction to Gödel's theorems. Cambridge University Press.
- The Constitution: A collection of historically important communications of the United States of America. (2014). Bendon.
- Tocqueville, A. de. (2004). Democracy in America (H. Reeve, Trans.). Bantam Dell.

- Whitehead, A. N. (1964). Science and philosophy. Littlefield, Adams & Co.
- Wills, G. (2008). Head and heart: A history of Christianity in America. Penguin Books Ltd.

Electronic Resources

- Library of Congress. (n.d.). Religion and the founding of the American Republic.Retrieved from: https://www.loc.gov/exhibits/religion/index.html
- Luther, M. (n.d.). Works of Martin Luther, with introductions and notes/Volume1/Disputation on Indulgences. Retrieved from https://en.wikisource.org/wiki/Works_of_Martin Luther, with_introductions_and_notes/Volume_1/Disputatio n_on_Indulgences#Ninety-fiveTheses
- Nietzsche, F. (n.d.). Thus spake Zarathustra: A book for all and none. Retrieved from: https://www.gutenberg.org/files/1998/1998h/199 8-h.htm#link2H_4_0006

Glossary of Terms

Historical/Political/Economic/Social Terminology

- **Absolutism**: In 16th and 17th century Europe the authority over the state by claimed divine monarchical rule. Involved military, political, and religious powers being beholden to the supreme authority of the ruler to uphold the existing hierarchy of the state.
- **Constitution of the United States of America**: The foundational document of American law. Includes the Bill of Rights. The first amendment outlines the limitations of government in matters of freedom conscience and freedom of expression.
- **Enlightenment**: In 17th and 18th century Europe there was a shift in mindset toward philosophical rationalism and scientific inquiry as guiding principles of human activity.
- **Laissez-Faire**: The relaxation of government interest in the affairs of citizens.
- **Marketplace of (Spiritual) Ideas**: The concept that in the absence of state-backed religion, spiritual belief systems must compete on their merits to gain influence and to prove their benefits for those who may be interested in subscribing to them.
- **Mercantilism**: State-directed commerce. During the 15th ~ 18th centuries, early modern European mercantilism emphasized colonial expansion and accumulation of state wealth under the premise that the world contains finite riches.
- **Merit System**: The idea that through free exchange of goods, services, ideas, and open discussion about such things leads to optimal benefit for a society.

- **Monarchism**: A governmental structure formed by hereditary claim to authority. The ruler in a monarchy typically directs the affairs of the state as has the final say in matters pertaining to state interest. While the shift in Europe has been away from rule by monarchical principles toward governance premised on democratic principles, many European countries to this day retain 'Kingdom' in their official name. Also, varying degrees of sentimentalism and civic pride regarding national monarchical heritage remain in many European countries.
- **Protestant Ethic**: A term used to describe the character of the late 19th and early 20th century American citizen. Coined by German Sociologist Max Weber (1864-1920) based on his observations upon visiting the United States in 1904 to conduct research on the development of American society.
- **Protestant Reformation**: A religious movement that took hold in 16th century Europe that destabilized the Catholic Church. It Emphasized the development of a personal relationship with God, individual engagement with the bible and scripture, which sought to bypass priestly interpretation of the bible on behalf of the individual.

Philosophical Terminology

- **Absurdism**: The theory that there is no meaning to be found in the universe.
- **Agnosticism**: Uncertainty regarding the existence of God.
- **Atheism**: A conviction of belief that God does not exist.
- **Existentialism**: A broad umbrella of philosophical inquiry under which the concerns for human experience and the state of human existence are examined and considered.

- **Humanism**: In Enlightenment Europe it emerged as an area of understanding premised on the rediscovery and reapplication of the work of classical Greek and Roman philosophers. In the modern branches of Humanism, some retain the Enlightenment premise, while others view the human condition as one of aloneness and struggle in a hostile universe.
- **Paradox**: An idea or statement of seeming internal contradiction lending itself to being absurd, not provable, or not true. *In current academic use, there is a move away from 'paradox' and toward reframing 'paradoxes' as 'unresolved' theorems.
- **Theorem**: a statement or proposition thought to be provable using supporting logic and theorems previously considered to be valid.

Philosophy of Mathematics Terminology

- **Algorithm**: In math, a sequence of operations or procedures applied to a series or set of numbers or axioms. *This type of process is thought to be transferable to philosophical reasoning through converting ideas or thoughts into axioms and then using algorithmic operations to experiment with the ideas and thoughts as axioms.
- **Axiom**: A stand-alone statement generally regarded to be true without necessity of substantiation.
- **Finite Mathematics**: A branch of mathematics that works with objects containing tangible, fixed, or limited properties.
- **Integer**: A wholly complete number and not a fraction or portion of a number.
- **Proof(s)**: Argumentation that supports the validity of a proposition.
- **Parametric Logic**: The classification and arrangement of ideas and properties of objects into

bound sets helps to provide definition and order to the limitlessness of infinite possibility.
- **Set Theory**: The idea of arranging ideas, objects, symbols into bounded collections.
- **Theorem**: See 'Philosophical Terminology'
- **Truism(s)**: A statement that is generally agreed upon to be true, such that it does not require any further clarification or further inquiry.
- **Undecidability**: When the validity of a proposition cannot be proven or unproven without being self-referential or self-contradictory.
- **Validity**: When a theorem gains acceptance through the reason or formal process as provable and its provability can be independently replicated.

Theological/Religious/Spiritual Terminology

- **Abrahamic Faith Tradition**: Name for the three largest monotheistic religions (Judaism, Christianity, Islam) that recognizes their shared heritage.
- **Absolution Theory**: The idea that God is not the cause of suffering and evil, but that suffering and evil are permissible by God.
- **Antinomianism**: The belief that adherence to spiritual or religious law is no longer necessary.
- **Apostolic Era**: The time immediately following the resurrection of Christ in which the Christian message was being spread for the Christian Church to become established. (Death of Christ ~ End of the 1st century AD).
- **Apologetics**: A systematic approach to defending one's faith. Christian or otherwise.
- **Apostolic Succession**: A claim to religious authority and governance by way of hereditary lineage dating back to the Apostles in the 1st century C.E.
- **Buddhism**: An eastern spiritual philosophy with roots in Hinduism.

Compossibility ~ Incompossibility Theory
- *A proposed description of, and proposed composition of the properties and principles of substance and ideas chosen from and used (or not used) by God in His creation.*

Standard and Expanded* Use of Compossible ~ Incompossible in the Destruction of Logic from Within
- *Compossible substance and ideas are favorable to God for creation because their properties contain no internal contradiction, and are thus deemed as being of excellent quality.*
- *Incompossible substance and ideas contain internally contradictory properties, and thus God does not choose from them for His creation because of their poor quality.*
- **For the purposes of the current volume, the usage of the compossible ~ incompossible paradigm has been expanded to include acts of free will by humans that are either compatible or incompatible with the goodness of God's creation.*
- ***Additionally, the usage has been expanded in this volume as a tool of analysis for the degree of consistency of seeming contradictory concepts presented in biblical scripture.*

Theological/Religious/Spiritual Terminology Continued
- **Compunction**: Feeling as though one must act from a place of spiritual or moral guilt or deficit.
- **Convergence ~ Divergence Theory**: An extension of the concept of spiritual formation. The idea that in moments such as birth and death a person's spirit is integrated with their physical body whereas at death their physical body and spirit part ways.
- **Exegetics**: An approach to interpreting scripture in the way it was intended to be understood at the time

it was written as best as possible in its original context.
- **Free Will**: An idea of conscience that people have the agency to determine their own outcomes in life.
- **Just (Divine) Compensation Theory**: The idea that a person must earn their way into Heaven through an accounting of their good deeds and transgressions while on earth.
- **Koans**: From the Buddhist tradition. Meditating to reflect on a semantic paradox or a more profound paradox. The objective is not to solve the contradiction but rather to sit with it in contemplation.
- **Liturgical Latin**: A type of official language used in Church. Contrasted using vernacular language in Church.
- **Merit Theology**: The idea that a person earns favor with God through good deeds.
- **Monotheism**: The belief that there is one supreme Deity or God.
- **Polytheism**: The belief that there are multiple Deities and Gods.
- **Predestination ~ Determinism**: The idea that because God is all-knowing and all- powerful, He has already decided the future for every individual and the fate of their soul upon dying.
- **Religious/Spiritual Intermediary**: A person who claims special divine knowledge or insight, acts as an interpreter of divine knowledge, and claims diplomacy and agency in human-divine relations.
- **Religiosity**: Over-investment in practices of religious custom with diminished awareness of the premise of the custom or the implications.
- **Secularism**: A lifestyle that relaxes, de-emphasizes, or does not involve religious practices.

- **Spiritual Formation**: The development of one's personal spiritual character and the process of spiritual maturation.
- **Spiritual Gatekeeping**: Used in conjunction with Religious or Spiritual Intermediary, used as a description of how the idea divine favor can be a tool of coercion.

Supplemental Practical Material I

Example of a Formal Logical Procedure

Formulation of Premise/Hypothesis

- Identify Idea or Problem to be Addressed
- Identity Main Idea/Actions if Necessary/Who Will Benefit
- Gathering Research/Preliminary Legwork Formulate the Premise
- Clarification and Refinement of Premise will be Ongoing

Application of 1st Order Logic

- Abductive Reasoning
- Analogous Reasoning
- Causal Reasoning
- Deductive Reasoning
- Inductive Reasoning
- Probabilistic Reasoning

Application of 2nd Order Logic: Substantive and Evidentiary

- Analogical Evidence
- Anecdotal Evidence
- Case Studies
- Hypothetical Evidence
- Statistical Evidence
- Testimonial Evidence
- Textual Evidence

Application of 3rd Order Logic: Ethical, Moral, Philosophical Contextualization of the Premise

- Moral Implications of Premise
- Ethical Implications of Premise
- Philosophical Implications of Premise
- Systemic or Interactional Implications between parts of Premise

Application of 4th Order Logic: Defense from Objections arising from Premise

- Evidential Refutation
- Logical Refutation
- Refutation via Discrepancy
- Refutation via Counterexample
- Refutation via Reduction to Extreme (Reductio ad Absurdum)
- Concessions/Deflections/Reframing as strategies in response to Objections

Pre-Conclusion Process

- Revisit and then Strengthen the Premise
- Synthesize/Integrate/Contextualize
- Bias Check/Review from External Party
- Review of Moral/Ethical Impact and Implications for those who will be affected by the initial premise
- Revise/Refine/Strengthen Premise
- Review/Implementation/Practical Application of Procedures

Conclusion of Formal Logic Procedure

- Offer Clarity on the Summary of Key Points, Next Steps, and Further Action

Supplemental Practical Material II

A Quick Glance at Kurt Gödel's Incompleteness Theorems (1931)

Theorem 1

Within any formal process of stating numbers or symbols (as part of a process of ordering a set of numbers, for example, listing a set of integers: 1, 2, 3, 4, 5,) there will be statements of symbols that cannot be proven or disproven within the set, and because of this, the set can not be proven to be consistent or complete and thus the set is of undecided validity.

(Adapted from: Crilly pg. 189 [see Works Cited] for the purpose of philosophical and theological application.)

Theorem 2

If a formal process of stating or ordering (again, stating and ordering of numbers or symbols as part of a set) is proven to be consistently valid, then its consistency necessitates external validation for the system itself to be of decided validity.

(Adapted from: Crilly pg. 189 [see Works Cited] for the purpose of philosophical and theological application.)

About Experiments in Christian Thought

Experiments in Christian Thought approaches Christian spirituality in unconventional ways to make the merits of Christian ideas better understood for people seeking answers to life's big questions.

In an age where the plausibility of God's existence is often rejected and even mocked reflexively on scientific grounds, this series will offer a second look at the topic of Christian spirituality.

To people who unquestioningly adhere to the 'conventional wisdom' in current academic institutions that God is, or ought to be an off-limits topic for any 'rational' minded person; this series is for you.

To the university or college student who finds themself saying 'trust the science', or 'the science says', the author offers this series as a gateway to bridging rigid philosophical rationalism with spiritual belief.

While exploring this series, the reader will see that despite progress in material well-being and other scientific advancements, human nature remains the same today as it has been throughout history. Any number of personal problems, experiences, or questions that a person has today have been experienced and asked by many people who have come and gone before the present time.

In the present age, people have a tendency toward kneejerk reactions to overturn, demolish, and reinvent anything that doesn't seem to fit with presupposed worldviews. To such people, it is as though humanity is in a perpetual state of crisis and the answer is to simply discredit the past with reckless abandon.

Drawing from pre-21st century wisdom, this series offers comfort to those who are ideological drifters with the assurance that in history, someone, somewhere, has likely experienced something very similar to the problems of today, personally and on a societal level.

Over the course of the series, Christian spirituality will show its compatibility with rationalism, and demonstrate that this mindset was the prevailing norm throughout much of history before the 20th century.

The series will also look to the future as to what Christian ministry and discipleship will mean with the prospect of sentient AI on the horizon.

Experiments in Christian Thought Volumes 1 & 2 are currently available in both Paperback and eBook editions.

Volumes 3 & 4 will be released at a later date.

Experiments in Christian Thought is Enthusiastically Brought To You By:

Idea Factory Press Scarborough, Canada.
https://www.ideafactorypress.com
We Make the Lights Come On!

Volumes 1, 2, 3, 4, of Experiments in Christian Thought are Copyrighted Material.
Copyright © Matthew M. Kryzanowski, 2024.
ALL RIGHTS RESERVED

About Idea Factory Press

Idea Factory Press is an independent publishing company from Toronto, Canada currently offering experimental non-fiction writing and sheet music.

Offerings from Idea Factory Press include paperback and e-book versions of the available catalog. Books are available through an assortment of vendors and libraries.

Idea Factory Press strives to create original paperback and eBook offerings based on freely generated ideas and thoroughly researched topics.

To stay updated and to learn about forthcoming books please visit:

https://www.ideafactorypress.com
https://www.linkedin.com/company/ideafactorypress

We make the lights come on!

About the Author

Matthew Kryzanowski was raised in Kingston Ontario, Canada. He has a background in music, and is a graduate of the Queen's University School of Music. Additionally, he has a degree in History and holds the designation of Ontario Certified Teacher. Matthew has been teaching since 2004 in Toronto. He has been married to his lovely wife for 16 years, and together they have two children. In addition to being an educator, Matthew has spent much of the last twenty years serving various local church communities by directing choirs and providing service music.

https://www.ideafactorypress.com
https://www.amazon.com/author/matthewmkryzanowski
https://www.librarything.com/author/kryzanowskimatthewm

More Books by Matthew M. Kryzanowski

The Compossible Pair: *G.W. Leibniz & Mary Baker Eddy*
Experiments in Christian Thought Volume 2
2nd English Edition (Revised & Expanded)

A Work of Experimental Christian Philosophy that Pushes Back Against Evil and Suffering

Paperback ISBN 978-1-0688629-1-5
eBook ISBN 978-1-0688629-5-3

The Compossible Pair: G.W. Leibniz & Mary Baker Eddy
2nd Edition (Revised & Expanded)

In the face of God as limitless in love, wisdom, and ability, it is justifiable to say that misery and suffering afflict humanity seemingly in perpetuity.

Yet, in the Christian ideation of God as an all-loving, all-knowing, and all-powerful entity, the response from such a God as Christians claim Him to be, is seen by many to be one of empty and chilling silence.

In this 2nd revised & expanded edition of **The Compossible Pair: *G.W. Leibniz & Mary Baker Eddy***, properties and principles of the metaphysical composition of the world as proposed by German Enlightenment era Mathematician and Philosopher, Gottfried Wilhelm Leibniz (1646-1716) are harmonized with the spiritual ontology of self as understood by Christian Experimentalist Theologian, Mary Baker Eddy (1821-1910).

In this meeting of compatible minds, **The Compossible Pair** seeks to advance understanding of the occurrence of suffering and evil in what is known as the "best possible world" that has been created for the good.

This original offering from Idea Factory Press argues that humanity's use of free will is an undecidable (but still good part of the created world) that tilts toward diminishment of the compossible and good within in each person, when not attended to, and when inflicted as harm upon others, degradation of the well-formed metaphysical properties and principles of the created world occur.

The Compossible Pair proposes when affliction is viewed as degradation of the compossible world, it can be seen as the mechanism by which proliferation of pain and suffering occur, and is therefore in contradiction to, and within the world created by God for the good.

By integrating G.W. Leibniz's and Mrs. Baker Eddy's compatibility of understanding human physical and spiritual experience, it is hoped the reader will find a fresh way to respond to the question:

If God; why evil?

In this work of experimental theology, the Christian view of God will be defended in the face of external criticism. The book does this by clarifying historical reasons for scriptural misunderstanding that have led to the perception and charge that the Bible is incoherent.

Copyright © Matthew M. Kryzanowski, 2025. All Rights Reserved.

Please do a web search for availability at your favorite bookstore or local library.

Thank You for Reading this Book!